MEMOIRS of a Doctor

An extraordinary journey of faith
across continents that will encourage, enlighten, and
empower you to fulfill your God-ordained destiny!

DR ANDREW C.S. KOH

Published in Malaysia by Dr. Koh Chan Sing, Andrew.
No. 21, Jalan Intan, Taman Intan, 31650 Ipoh, Perak.
Email: changsingkoh@gmail.com

ISBN: 978-967-18409-9-3

Printed in Malaysia by Akitiara Corporation Sdn. Bhd.

Design, Layout & Editing by Ramesh Rudd

Foreword

Memoirs of a Doctor is the story of Dr. Andrew C.S. Koh's faith journey through life from his humble childhood in Tanjong Malim until his retirement in Ipoh in 2020. He comes from a very poor background, from a very small and insignificant town in Malaysia. Although Andrew's parents were non-Christians, God had sown the seed of gospel message into his heart as early as primary school, in the chapel service through the story of the prodigal son.

Through education, he got out of poverty, left Tanjong Malim, and made it good by becoming a medical doctor, a heart specialist, and an internal medicine specialist. He was born again as a Christian in his medical student days and some years later while working in Telok Intan, he rededicated his life to Jesus Christ.

On returning to Ipoh, he was mentored by two prominent Bible teachers who taught him the whole counsel of God expositionally from Genesis to Revelation.

I was fortunate enough to be his pastor for about 10 years when he worked at the Ipoh Specialist Hospital and worshiped at the Holy Cross Lutheran Church, Ipoh where I was pastoring. Over the years, Andrew and his family become our family friends as well.

Andrew earnestly prayed for his patients before subjecting them to any medical procedure. His medical profession was a "tent-making" ministry to share the gospel to non-Christians as a market place soul winner. It was also a platform to encourage and pray for Christians who needed his services.

He loved the Lord, studied, preached, and taught the Bible. In the course of his medical practice, he helped a lot of people in need, both medically and spiritually. He also preached in the Holy Cross Lutheran Church periodically when I was pastoring there.

In 1999, upon God's calling, he took a 3-year sabbatical from practicing medicine to study full-time in Laidlaw Bible College in Auckland New Zealand from 1999 to 2001. Memoirs of a Doctor traces his journey of faith all the way from childhood until his retirement in January 2020.

It is an inspiring story of how God works in the life of a person who is faithful, obedient, and surrendered to His calling. It is about how God can use a person as His chosen instrument in the Kingdom.

This book will be a great inspiration to many readers, particularly to those who are just starting out their journey in life. It will no doubt be a legacy to his wife, three sons, three daughters-in-law, 5 grandsons, 4 granddaughters, and future generations. I wish him all the best in his golden years as he continues his ministry as an author, lay preacher, bible teacher, bible expositor, blogger, poet, musician, soul winner, traveler, etc.

Pastor Paul Chong & Mrs. Ame Chong,
London, United Kingdom.
January 2021

Preface

This is a memoir of my life from childhood until retirement. The recollection of my childhood details remain sketchy as the events happened more than half a century ago.

The purpose of this book is to document the story of my life as a legacy for my family members, relatives, friends, colleagues, and future generations to read, keep, treasure, and be inspired.

Writing this memoir had been on my mind for at least 5 years but due to work commitments, I did not have the time nor energy to do it. My retirement in January 2020 gave me the time, motivation, and impetus to complete this project.

In retrospect, writing this memoir was easier than I thought, and the experience gained was very enriching. It only took me slightly more than one month to progress from blank page to draft manuscript stage. However, editing and proofreading took a much longer time.

I wish to dedicate this book to my late grandfather, Koh Tuck, my late father, Koh Kam Sang, my late mother, Wu Choh Lan, my late uncle Wu Cheok Lim, my beloved wife, Cheah Wai Yin, my sons, Joseph, Joshua, Joel, my daughters-in-law, Renee, Tina, Angelina, my grandsons, Isaac, Benjamin, Daniel, Josiah, Jonathan, my granddaughters, Giselle, Katie, Annabelle, and Isabelle.

I thank God for giving me such a fulfilling life and for preserving me through so many dangerous situations. I wish to thank my daughter-in-law Tina for her encouragement and support, without which this book would have never seen the light of day.

My thanks to Dr. Tim Sng, Canon Dr. S.K. Teoh, book writing coach – Sister Ruth Saw, Pastor Peggy Seow, Pastor Joshua Tan, sister Joanna Lee, my school teachers, the late Mrs. Jothi, the late Mr. Abel, the late Mr. Nagappan, my high school teacher Dato K.R.R Naidu, my high school classmate Lim Soo Ken, my medical school classmate Dato Dr. Gunasegaran, and others for their suggestions.

Last but not least, I wish to thank everyone who has contributed to this book in one way or another.

Dr. Andrew C.S. Koh
Ipoh, Malaysia.
January 2021

MEMOIRS

A TALE OF TWO CITIES,
TANJONG MALIM AND AUCKLAND

A TALE OF TWO COUNTRIES,
MALAYSIA AND NEW ZEALAND

A TALE OF TWO TENSES,
THE PAST AND THE PRESENT

A TALE OF TWO LIVES,
THE FLESH AND SPIRITUAL

A TALE OF TWO PROFESSIONS,
CARDIOLOGY AND THEOLOGY

A TALE OF LOVE AND PROVIDENCE,
PERSISTENCE AND PERSEVERANCE

WALKING AND SURRENDERING,
TO THE GLORY OF GOD.

Synopsis

Memoirs of a Doctor is the story my life this far. This story began from my birthday on 11th January 1952 until my retirement day on 11th Jan 2020. The purpose of my memoir is to document my life story as a legacy for my family, relatives and friends.

The story traces back to the tough beginnings of the 1950s when life and society was very backward – when industrialization, computerization, and automation was unheard of.

Life was slow and leisurely, letters were sent and read through the postal service, and communication was slow, and perhaps inefficient by today's pace. This book is divided into 8 chapters, each chapter describing a particular stage of my life, with photos relevant to each chapter and a poem before each chapter.

The story unfolds with each chapter and culminates with the testimony of my retirement in 2020. There are certainly many valuable life lessons to be learnt from a story covering a span of so many years. If any reader is inspired to trust in God, excel in life, and persevere in the face of adversity, this book would have achieved its purpose.

Contents

NOSTALGIC MEMORIES

MES CLASS OF 69

42 years went by, in the blink of an eye,
Grand reunion by the riverside,
Brought back memories of years gone by.

Memories of boy scouts and girl guides,
Came scurrying by,
Emotions running high.

Karaokes, dances, wines, and dines,
To keep the night alive,
Thank you for the nostalgic night,
Of yesteryears gone by.

CHAPTER ONE

GROWING UP IN *TANJUNG MALIM*

"It was the best of times, it was the worst of times"

- A Tale of Two Cities, Charles Dickens.

I belong to the baby boomer generation. My life story began in the year 1952 when I was born in Tanjong Malim – a very small, insignificant town in the Mualim District of Perak in Malaysia. It is located 70 km to the north of Kuala Lumpur and 120 km to the south of Ipoh, sitting on the Perak-Selangor border, where the Ulu Bernam River provides its natural dividing line.

IF NOT FOR THE GRACE OF GOD

According to my parents, I was born in a shophouse where they lived. In those days medical facilities were poor and so was transportation. There was no ambulance service, and my parents did not own a car. My mother did not have enough time to rush me to the hospital when she went into labour pain.

So I was born at home and my delivery was assisted by my mother's friend who happened to be there at the time. My mother was very grateful for this and they became best of friends ever since. On looking back, I'm convinced that it was God who rescued me. If not for the grace of God, I certainly would not be around to tell you my story.

PRAISE THE STARS

My grandfather being the patriarch of the family was assigned the task of giving me a name. He came up with the name, Chan Sing which means, "praise the stars" in Cantonese. *Chan* means to praise, and *Sing* means stars. According to my grandfather, I was born on a night when there were plenty of stars in the sky.

So he praised the stars and called me Chan Sing. To him, I was one of those twinkling little stars in the dark starry night. This reminded me of the Vincent Van Gogh's song, starry, starry night. So this was how I came into this world and how I got my name.

The origin of my name reminds me of the story of Abraham (Abram) in the book of Genesis. God promised Abraham that He would bless him with posterity:

"The Lord had said to Abram, "Go from your country, your people and your father's household to the land I will show you. I will make you into a great nation, and I will bless you. I will make your name great, and you will be a blessing. I will bless those who bless you, and whoever curses you I will curse, and all peoples on earth will be blessed through you." – Genesis 12: 2-3

However, after many years went by and still not having any offspring, Abraham was worried. So one day, God appeared to Abraham in a vision and gave him a promise that his descendants would be as numerous as the stars in the night sky:

He took him outside and said, "look up at the sky and count the stars if indeed you can count them." Then he said to him, "so shall your offspring be" – Genesis 15:5

UNIQUENESS OF TANJUNG MALIM

Tanjong Malim is a unique town sitting at the border between two states. One half of the town is in the state of Perak and the other half is in Selangor, divided right across the middle by the Ulu Bernam River. Back in those days, even the water in the river was unique. One half of the river was clear while the other half was muddy – clear on the Perak side and murky on the Selangor side.

The town is famous for its Yik Mun Pau or dumplings, made by the Yik Mun family, which is still available today. Tanjong Malim is also home to the famous Sultan Idris Teacher's Training College, inaugurated in 1922, now called the Sultan Idris Education University, and the RM 1.8 billion Proton City township, which houses the Proton car assembly plant, established in 1996.

MY GRANDFATHER

My grandfather came from China in the 1940s from a town called Sei Wooi in the Guang Doong district. He had two sons in China but for some reason, he came to Malaysia with only one son, my father, and my grandfather's wife.

Unfortunately, his younger son, my father's younger brother was left behind in China under the care of relatives. So my father did not have any siblings in Malaysia. My grandmother passed away before I was even born so I do not know anything about her.

My grandfather was a cobbler. He operated a one-man business, repairing and restoring shoes. However due to alcoholism and opium addiction he was always living in poverty. He was a kind-hearted man and I loved him very dearly.

I remember him taking me to the barber whenever my hair grew a little too long for his liking. He always told the barber to cut my hair really short much to my anguish. My grandfather passed away eventually due to old age. His death had a profound effect on me because this was the first time that I experienced the loss of someone really close to me.

MY MOTHER

My mother originated from another town in Perak called Bidor. She came from a rich family background. Her father owned land and plantations in Bidor. She was third in a family of six siblings comprising of two boys and four girls. She was her father's favourite daughter. My parents met through matchmaking as this was the custom in those days. As alien as it is today, people in those days did not usually fall in love and choose their spouses. Their parents chose life partners and arranged their marriage for them.

NO. 22, CHONG AH PENG STREET

My parents owned a tinsmith shop at number 22, Chong Ah Peng Street, which was located in the town center. This shop was still there in its original condition until 2019, when it was torn down and rebuilt. I was fortunate enough to do a photoshoot of this shophouse in 2018 with the 7 of us who lived here in 1958.

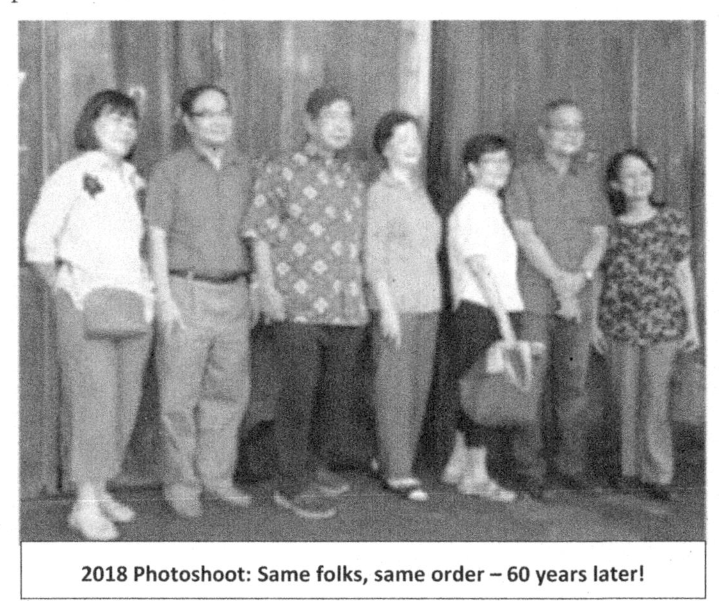

2018 Photoshoot: Same folks, same order – 60 years later!

It was divine providence, grace, and a miracle that brought us back together for a grand reunion in Tanjong Malim for this historic and rare photoshoot in 2018.

Back then, we were all kids, and I was only 6 years old when we had our photographs taken. For the 2018 photoshoot, every one of us stood in front of the shop according to our same positions as in the 1958 photograph.

1958 Photoshoot: The Original – Six decades ago!

TOUGH BEGINNINGS

I am the youngest in a family of 4 siblings, 3 boys and 1 girl. I have 2 elder brothers and 1 elder sister. My second brother passed away peacefully in his sleep in Singapore in 2009 at the age of 59 years. I am now left with 1 elder brother and 1 elder sister.

My late parents were very poor when they were in Tanjong Malim. The tinsmith business was slow, and trading was very difficult. Malaysia was in a deep recession then and the economy was extremely bad. They were always in debt, living a hand to mouth existence. They were Taoists who were deeply steeped in idolatry and ancestor worship.

Growing up in Tanjong Malim was very tough for me due to poverty in extremis. Malaysia and the rest of the world was in a deep recession. Tin, rubber, and commodity prices were at all-time lows. We could not afford many things. Even the purchase of food and sundry supplies were on credit. My family was one of the poorest families in Tanjong Malim.

We lived in a rented shophouse. My father rented half the shop downstairs and one of the rooms upstairs. The remaining rooms upstairs were rented out to other tenants. The other half of the shop was rented out to a car and motorcycle repair shop which was very noisy and dirty. The place that we were living in was not conducive for any form of study.

THE CURFEW

I remember that there was once a curfew in Tanjong Malim. I think it must have been during the time of the Malayan Communist Party insurgency. We could not go out of the house at certain times of the day. We were under curfew and locked down. It was much worse than the present COVID-19 pandemic lockdown.

I can still vividly remember my late father cooking pigeons for lunch and dinner. In those days, we had pigeons in the house. They flew in by themselves and when we fed them, more would come.

My late parents also reared chicken, ducks, geese, and turkeys. Every Christmas, my parents would give turkeys as Christmas presents to the estate manager who was our client. We also planted vegetables for own consumption. Even though my parents were poor, they provided for all their children's needs. In fact, I don't ever remember us starving or lacking food at any time.

GOOD TIMES IN BIDOR

I spent a significant proportion of my childhood days in Bidor where I had many cousins, especially during the school holidays. My cousins were the children of my mother's elder brother, and her elder and younger sisters. We had such good times playing games that children played back in those days like marbles, catapult, spiders, fighting fish, tops, kites, and so on. The distance from Tanjong Malim to Bidor is only 62 km or 45 minutes' drive by car. I used to take a bus on my own from Tanjong Malim to Bidor.

My late "big uncle", my mother's elder brother was especially good to me because I was good in my studies. He bought many brand-new watches for me. In those days, watches were considered expensive items. He was a very good saxophonist often playing in the house, in weddings, funerals, and other private functions. He could not read music, but played extremely well by ear. He was Bidor's equivalent of Kenny G.

My uncle worked as a projector operator in a movie cinema theatre. Often, he would take me and my cousins to watch movies in the theatre free of charge! Chinese New Years were almost always spent in Bidor and we played fire crackers and received Angpows from all the uncles and aunties. My auntie, big uncle's wife, would buy breakfast and supper every day for the children without fail.

I remember a massive flood occurring in Tanjong Malim in 1971. The whole town was flooded, and the water was up to waist level in our shop. The flood took several days to subside, and it badly damaged our furniture and office equipment. Cleaning up after the flood was in itself a great big undertaking!

IMPETUS TO SUCCEED

My parents were very superstitious, believing strongly in traditional Chinese medical care and healing by mediums. They were also very involved in Chinese temple worship. This childhood background spurred me on to get a good education to free myself from the bondage of poverty and get a better quality of life.

It also gave me the ambition to become a doctor at a very young age. I wanted to treat sick people based on proper medical science and not based on a superstitious belief system. The two local general practitioners near my late father's shop became my role models.

According to my parents, when I was a baby, I was very sick with measles, had high fever, dehydration, and almost died. But miraculously the fever resolved, and I survived. God was there again to preserve my life so that I am now able to tell you my story.

SCHOOL DAYS

I studied in the Methodist English Primary School from 1959 until 1964 and moved over to the Methodist English Secondary School from 1965 until 1969. I do not remember very much about my primary school years. However, I do remember that on my first day at school, my parents secretly put onions and sugar canes into my school bag. They believed that onions would make me intelligent because *"onion"* in Cantonese means *"intelligent"*.

They also believed that sugar cane will make me sweet because sugar cane is sweet. When one of my classmates opened my bag and saw the onions and sugar cane, he laughed and laughed until I did not know where to hide my face anymore.

This same classmate became my best friend in primary school, and we did many things together. We read books in the library and tuned in to the radio together for pop songs from performers like Cliff Richard, Shadows, Beatles, Herman's Hermits, Bread, Air Supply, Monkees, Marmalade and so on.

He combed his hair high, like his idol, the late king of pop, Elvis Presley. He also idolized Mary Poppins, and so he called himself Poppy Leong. We played tops, catapult, marbles, caught fighting fish from rivers and spiders from trees, flew kites, rode bicycles, played games, and participated in the Boy Scout movement.

One day I was very sad when my best friend suddenly left the school without informing me and I never got to see him again. I did not have a chance to say goodbye to him and did not have any closure. I remembered him telling me that he might have to follow his parents to Seremban someday, but did not give me any forwarding address.

I lost touch with him until 2015, after a lapse of 48 years, when we were united again thanks to Facebook, Google, WhatsApp, e-mail, and social media. He is now living in Jakarta and I have visited Jakarta twice just to meet up with him. The last time we met, he had forgotten about onions, sugar canes, Elvis Presley hairstyle, and

Mary Poppins. To my amazement, he did not even remember calling himself Poppy Leong back in those days!

ENCOUNTERING THE GOSPEL

When I was in primary school, there was a free period every Friday morning, where students were free to do whatever they wished. During this free period, I liked to attend the chapel service in the school church. I remember on one of those Friday morning chapel services, my class teacher, the late Mrs. Jothi told the class about the parable of the prodigal son from Luke 15:11-32, in the most masterly manner:

A man had two sons. The elder one was good and the younger was bad. The younger son took his share of his father's inheritance, left the town, and squandered all his money on wild living until he was bankrupt and had to feed pigs.

When this prodigal son came back to his senses, he returned to his father's house. To everyone's surprise, the father welcomed him back with open arms and hosted a grand feast to celebrate his return. In this parable, the father represented God. The prodigal son represented those who had run away from God, but God never gave up on them.

Although I was a free thinker, the parable of the prodigal son had a deep impact on me and got me thinking about God.

ROLE MODEL BROTHER

I was passionately involved in the Boy Scouts movement and participated in all their activities. The movement instilled good leadership fundamentals in me. My elder brother, Chan Wing, who was 2 years older than me was a King Scout. He was also a Head Prefect, my role model and mentor – a student who was highly regarded by his teachers and scout masters.

Chan Wing inspired me to excel in the Boy Scout Movement. We were inseparable and I learned a lot from him. The scout masters who were impressed by my brother's achievements within the movement also nurtured and trained me too.

THE SCOUT'S JOURNEY

My journey as a scout started off as a Private. I worked my way up the ladder by passing tests and accumulating badges. The first badge, the Tenderfoot was relatively easy to pass but subsequent badges got incrementally harder.

Scout's Photo – I'm the third one from the left

A scout must be able to tie different kinds of knots, identify trees, birds and flowers. Our swimming, hiking, trekking and jungle survival skills are also tested. The final hurdle is to get the King Scout badge. As for me, after a lot of hard work, as well as guidance from my scout master, I finally became a King Scout.

SUNGEI BILL CAMPSITE

I always looked forward to scout campfires, camping, and other activities. Camping was the highlight of my scouting days. Our camp site was in Sungei Bill – named after a river with the same name.

On arrival at the camp site, we would set up our tents. We had to dig a drain around the tent in case it rained. A single tent could accommodate up to four persons. There were many large, rounded rocks in the middle of the river emerging above the water.

For dinner, the senior scouts would boil rice and cook curry chicken with potatoes. They would also fry mee and mee hoon (rice noodles and vermicelli), and so on under the supervision of our scout masters.

As I remember, the boy scout's chicken curry rice was most yummy. I can still picture the spectacular scene – sitting on top of one of the large rocks while eating dinner and watching the beautiful scenery. The soothing sounds of the running river and the nearby waterfall encapsulated perfect peace.

Dinner would be followed by the campfire, whereby we sing songs, strum guitars, play games, share testimonies and so forth. "It Only Takes a Spark" and "Kumbayah" were among the favourite campfire songs back then.

At night, we had to do sentry duties, taking turns to guard the campsite in case there were any intruders namely wild boars, tigers, or other four-legged "friends". Fortunately, we did not encounter any snakes, but leeches and mosquitoes were plentiful. On some nights when we were lucky, could see owls with their two eyes peering at us through the night.

Scouts Group Photo – I'm the sixth one from the left [Standing]

To stay awake, we drank thick black coffee all night long. We kept the campfire burning both for warmth and to keep mosquitos and bugs away. Our Wellington boots adequately kept the leeches at bay while we patrolled the campsite carrying our torches on our rounds.

The symphony of sounds of the jungle at night was unique and entertaining. The majestic night sky with the moon and myriads of stars, showcasing Almighty God's dynamic painting.

SECONDARY SCHOOL

I was not much of an athlete and not particularly talented in sports. To compensate for this deficiency, I worked really hard academically. I was good in my studies, consistently finishing top of the class. This resulted in me being regularly chosen by the teachers to be prefect, class monitor, and also selected for other prominent academic roles.

In fact, as I remember, almost every year, I would be awarded book prizes and cash awards which made my parents happy and proud.

In secondary school, I did a lot of things which I should not have done. I remember going hitchhiking twice with another boy scout, once to Penang and another time to Melaka. This was to fulfill the requirement to attain the King Scout badge.

I did not have much cash in my pocket. I also did not inform my parents because they would not have allowed it. I used to go swimming in the Simpang Empat river with friends without informing my parents.

On one occasion, I had leg cramps while swimming and almost drowned. I screamed for help and someone pulled me out of the water just in time before I went under! Looking back, it was God again who saved my life. As far as I can remember, this was the third time God saved my life up to that point.

PETS & HOBBIES

I had pets too. They say the dog is man's best friend. From my experience, this is very true. I had a dog, called Bobby, a mongrel. I brought him home when he was just a puppy. He was a loyal, friendly, playful dog and I liked him a lot. But as he was growing up, he needed a lot of attention and care.

When I realised that I did not have the time to look after him properly, I gave Bobby away to a farmer. I blindfolded him and took him to the new owner's lorry and Bobby was transported to his farm in another town.

Two weeks later, to my surprise, Bobby came back to me, dirty, hungry, thirsty, and exhausted. I broke down in tears when I saw him. I was so heartless to send him away, but he faithfully came back to me. Ever since that day, I looked after Bobby until he died.

I also had two monkeys, one a male and the other one a female. The male one was called "Abang", but I cannot recall the name of the female monkey – talk about exotic pets! I liked reading the novels of William Shakespeare, Robert Louis Stevenson, Mark Twain, Charles Dickens, Enid Blyton and so on.

One day after reading the book Robinson Crusoe, I built a treehouse at the back of my father's shophouse. Every night, I would climb up into my treehouse to read books. This was my secret hiding place.

OTHER RECOLLECTIONS

I remember an incident where a Malay lady was swallowed alive by a crocodile when she was washing clothes and bathing in Ulu Bernam river. Everyone in the town was shocked over this incident.

Another heart-wrenching incident was that of a passenger whose head was severed when he popped his head out from the train as the train was passing through a bridge.

The sides of the bridge were very close to the window of the train. After this incident, someone pretended to be a ghost and frightened the people living near the train station. Fortunately, the police caught him, arrested and charged him in court.

Then there was the sad incident of the May 13, 1969 when riots broke out in Kuala Lumpur and many people lost their lives. Thankfully, Tanjong Malim was peaceful and did not have any riot or civil disturbance.

In 1969, when I was in Form 5, a fire broke out in Behrang Station, a satellite town near Tanjong Malim. A whole row of shops in the town center were burnt to the ground. I remember accompanying one of my friends to his house after school.

He was still in school uniform when he reached home to find his house completely destroyed. Fortunately, his family members were able to run out to safety in time before the fire engulfed their home.

I used to cycle from Tanjong Malim to Kalumpang, and from Tanjong Malim to Behrang Ulu and Behrang station to visit my classmates who lived there. We cycled in a group so that we could chit chat all the way.

When cycling from Behrang Ulu and Behrang Station to Tanjong Malim, we had to pass through a graveyard which was near the main road. Whenever we passed through this graveyard, it was always late in the evening. I remember us cycling really fast within the graveyard area for fear of devils coming after us!

There was also the incident where an Indian scout master in his forties disappeared suddenly and was never seen again. Even his family members did not know what happened to him. It was postulated that he was kidnapped by communist insurgents and killed in the jungle somewhere.

On the music front, I was active in a band called the Asteroid where I was the lead guitarist. It was a 5-piece band, with a singer, a drummer, a lead guitarist, a rhythm guitarist, and a bass guitarist. We were invited to play in the annual school talent-time, weddings, and private functions.

This band was partially reunited when three of us got together as a 3-piece band in our MES class of 69 annual reunions in 2018 and 2019. Sadly, one of the other guitarists, a former classmate of mine, passed away in 2020 due to liver cancer.

MES Band – I'm in the middle playing the Lead Guitar

SOJOURN IN KUALA LUMPUR

After the Form 5 school certificate examination in 1969, I had to wait for several months before the results could be announced. During this period, I went to Kuala Lumpur with a group of friends to work in a bakery in Pudu Road. I remembered we were being exploited by the company. They paid us peanuts and made us work long hours.

We started work at 8 am and worked until 10 pm, after a breakfast, a lunch break, a dinner break, and two tea breaks thrown in between. Breakfast and tea breaks were always tea with bread and kaya. It was nice to eat the bread that I baked through blood, sweats and tears. After finishing work, we slept in the worker's quarters within the bakery complex.

I made some good friends in the bakery. I remember this handsome boy, who took a liking to a beautiful girl who lived in the neighbourhood. The girl liked him too, but they had a wide chasm between them. The boy was uneducated, and the girl was educated. The boy was poor, and the girl was middle class.

They were from diametrically opposite backgrounds. He dated her on Sundays, which was our weekly rest day. The last I heard was that it did not work out for them. After the bakery stint, the boy left Kuala Lumpur, broke off with the girl he loved, and became a drug addict. I was very sad to hear about this.

THE STORY CONTINUES

This was my first experience with working life and earning my own salary. It was the first time I left Tanjong Malim, and the first time I lived in the big capital city of Malaysia called Kuala Lumpur. When the results were announced and I was told that I passed, I left the bakery job immediately and returned to Tanjong Malim.

I left Tanjong Malim in 1969 to continue my Form 6 education in Telok Intan, another town in Perak, 86 km away. After leaving Tanjong Malim, I lost contact with almost all of my Methodist English School Tanjong Malim (MESTM) classmates except for those who were selected to study in Telok Intan.

In 2015, through Facebook, Googles, WhatsApp, e-mail, and social media we were able to reconnect and formed the MESTM Class of 69 common interest WhatsApp chat group. This culminated in the first grand reunion in Shah Alam Club in 2016, followed by three more annual reunions in 2017, 2018, and 2019.

A smaller sub-group within the larger group also made several overseas trips to Perth, Jakarta, Medan, Lake Toba, and Vietnam. We also have yearly gatherings during Christmas, Chinese New Year, Hari Raya, Deepavali, and birthdays. However, our activities were curtailed in 2020 due to COVID 19 pandemic but we're looking forward to continuing our activities once the haze lifts.

ODE TO FRIENDS

HMSS CLASS OF 70

40 years after leaving the city,
Telok Intan by the sea.
Participants came back for a
reunion,
Involving many nations.

Memories came flooding back,
Unable to hold the emotions back.
Give me more songs and wines,
Karaoke, dance and dines.

Into the dead of the night,
Thank you for the nostalgic magic,

CHAPTER TWO

FORM SIX IN *TELOK INTAN*

"It was the age of wisdom, it was the age of foolishness, it was the epoch of belief, it was the epoch of incredulity, it was the season of light, it was the season of darkness, it was the spring of hope, it was the winter of despair."

– A Tale of Two Cities, Charles Dickens.

The next chapter of my life transported me to a small town called Telok Intan. I spent two years in Telok Intan from 1970 to 1971, pursuing an upper secondary education in the Horley Methodist Secondary School, HMSS. This was a 2-year course, the first year, in lower form 6 and second year, in upper form 6.

TELOK INTAN

Telok Intan is a medium-sized town in the Lower Perak district of Perak with a total population of 128,179 in 2016. The town was first called Telok Mak Intan or Mak Bay, but was later changed to Telok Anson (Anson Bay). After a third name change in 1982, it is now known as Telok Intan or Diamond Bay.

It is predominantly an agricultural township with many unique colonial buildings. Amongst these buildings is the famous leaning tower of Telok Intan, a pagoda-shaped building with a clock tower frontage, standing proudly at 25.5 meters, and tilting ominously leftward. This is the Malaysian equivalent of the world-famous Leaning Tower of Pisa in Italy.

In my first year at Telok Intan, I stayed with the family of my aunt –my mother's younger sister, which included my uncle, auntie and my cousins. They provided me with meals and accommodation and took very good care of me.

The next year, I shifted out to a homestay with another family which was nearer to the school. The environment in my new place was more conducive for studies as my other classmates were also staying in that area. I also needed the freedom, independence, and autonomy to be on my own.

MY TIME AT HMSS

HMSS had a long history dating back to 1899. It was founded by the Reverend W. E. Horley, who also founded the Anglo-Chinese School, Ipoh, in 1895. HMSS provided me with a good overall pre-University education.

HMSS Telok Intan Lower 6 Bio Class 1970 (I'm at 2nd Row, Extreme Right)

The teachers were very friendly, respectable, knowledgeable, helpful, and dedicated. About ten of my classmates from MES Tanjong Malim joined me in HMSS Telok Intan. Some female students from Convent School Telok Intan as well as students from the neighbouring towns of Tapah, Bidor, and Sungkai also joined us in HMSS, Telok Intan.

My memories of Telok Intan are quite vague as I don't remember very much of my time there. I was a School Prefect and

President of the 6th Form society. Among other things, we published monthly 6th Form Society newsletters and yearly magazines.

My best friend in Telok Intan was a student one year my junior. He was a top student from Bidor who joined HMSS in 1971. We were roommates in the same homestay. He was quite a joker, tall, fair, handsome, intelligent – a ladies' man.

We did a lot of things together. Printing the 6th Form society newsletters, playing games, cycling, listening to music, doing outdoor activities, and so on. By this time, I had passed the age for tops, marbles, catapult, fighting fish, flying kites and spiders – the stuff I did back in primary school.

REAL INTERACTION SANS SOCIAL MEDIA

In those days, we did not have internet, mobile phones, tablets, e-mail, WhatsApp, Google, and so forth. We directly communicated person to person, and face to face. We had a lot more human interaction. Life was much simpler then and so carefree. We did not carry baggage like adults do. Our stoic philosophical motto was, "eat drink and be merry, for tomorrow we die". We did not have to make prior appointments just to meet up. All meetings were more or less ad-hoc and spontaneous.

I still enjoyed playing the guitar on my own but did not join any band. In fact, I did not join the Boy Scout movement in HMSS, opting instead to practice Tae Kwon-Do in the evenings. I did play some games but did not particularly excel in any sports or athletics. Nevertheless, I was a good and conscientious student. I did well in my studies, and was one of the top students.

TRAGEDY IN 1970

I remember one tragic incident in 1970 when one of my classmates committed suicide by hanging himself in his house. He suffered from depression but did not seek medical advice. A few weeks earlier, he shared with me that he was a failure, unpopular and did not excel in his studies. He even felt that no one liked him as he was not voted into any prominent position in any society.

This individual said that he envied my popularity and wished he could be in my shoes. He had a look of sadness and depression on his face. A few days before the incident, he was seen walking around the neighborhood carrying some ropes with him. The whole school was shocked when it happened.

Nobody, including me, expected him to take his own life even though all the telltale signs were there. On hindsight, I think that I should have been more caring and assisted him in seeking medical advice. Perhaps then, the tragedy could have been averted but it was too late.

GOSPEL SEED SOWN

There was a classmate who had become a Christian in HMSS Telok Intan. He was friendly, honest, caring, and warm, a good role model. He shared the gospel and the love of God with me. He invited me to Christian fellowships. I attended many of these meetings, enjoyed the sharing, friendship, and refreshments.

The seed of the gospel was sown into my heart even though I did not believe. At that time, my heart could be considered as an indifferent or hardened heart. The message did not take root and did not grow. It was a "one ear in and one ear out" situation. Still I am forever thankful for his friendship.

Another one of my classmates developed schizophrenia in the second year. He became very religious and started telling everyone that he was Jesus Christ and had come to save the world. Over the next few months, he became more and more psychotic and could not continue his studies.

On hindsight, I should have taken him to seek medical advice as schizophrenia is treatable and can be controlled. After some time, he left the school, and I do not know what happened to him after that.

JELLYFISH ENCOUNTER

I loved the annual nature study trips organised by a pleasant Chinese lady science teacher. In the second year, or upper sixth, she took our class to an island resort called Pulau Sembilan for a nature study excursion. We spent 3 days and 2 nights there to study the fauna and flora of the island resort. The beach and the seaside were very beautiful and relaxing.

All of us enjoyed the assignments, camaraderie, fellowship, and returned with great memories of the outing. I remember one of my legs getting stung by a jellyfish and becoming swollen. Thankfully, the swelling subsided rather quickly and uneventfully.

MEETING MY HELPMEET

I needed some extra income to pay for my homestay. So I thought of giving private tuitions. Behind the scenes, and without my knowledge, God answered my prayer in His unique and benevolent way.

One day, a pleasant Chinese girl from the Convent School approached me and asked whether I could give private home tuition to a Form 4 student. I said "yes" and that was how I started to give tuition to the girl for 2 years. Little did I know that this girl would eventually become my wife.

HAND OF PROVIDENCE

My time in Telok Intan culminated with me sitting for the Higher School Certificate Examination, HSCE. The result of this examination determines whether one will make it to university or not. I did very well in the HSCE and was accepted into the reputable Medical School at the University of Malaya, Kuala Lumpur, where the late Professor Emeritus Tan Sri T. J. Danaraj was the Dean.

I was also awarded a Perak State Scholarship that paid all my tuition fees and cost of living allowances for the entire 5-years duration of my course from 1972-1977. The scholarship was indeed God-sent. My parents were poor and would never have been able to finance my University education. Even though I was still a free thinker, God provided for me through the scholarship. God's providence was at work in my life.

I remember that one of the interviewers for the scholarship interview was my father's friend, who was a member of the Parliament of Tanjong Malim, the late Mr. Lee Seck Fun. During the interview, he was very friendly, gentle and immediately put me at ease. He asked very simple questions that I had no difficulty in answering! After the interview he told me that I would be getting the scholarship and all I had to do was to wait for the result.

After the announcement of the HSCE examination results and the awarding of the Perak State Scholarship, I had to wait 6 months before the University of Malaya Semester started in July 1972. So I went to Ipoh and stayed with my sister and brother-in-law for several months. At this juncture, they had already become Christians for several years – a radical shift from their previous non-Christian background.

When I was alone in the house, I regularly took the Bible and started reading the gospels – Matthew, Mark, Luke and John. Although I was still a free thinker, the Bible spoke to me and left a deep impression in my heart. The seed of the gospel was again sown into my heart.

After leaving Telok Intan, I lost contact with my HMSS classmates until 2016, when some of us were reunited thanks to Facebook, Google, WhatsApp, e-mail and social media. We still communicate through WhatsApp and Facebook. Unfortunately, to this day, I still cannot trace many of my ex-HMSS mates.

MEMORIES OF YESTERYEARS

MU CLASS OF 72

39 years after leaving medical school,
Doctors from many nations,
Came back to the same station.
Memories came flooding back,
Unable to hold our emotions back.

Singing, dancing, drinking, and dining,
Into the dead of the night,
Thank you for the nostalgic night,
Of yesteryears gone by.

Andrew C.S. Koh ©2021

CHAPTER THREE

MEDICAL UNDERGRADUATE

UNIVERSITY MALAYA

"A dream, all a dream, that ends in nothing, and leaves the sleeper where he lay down, but I wish you to know that you inspired it."

- A Tale of Two Cities, Charles Dickens.

I spent the next 6 years of my life in Kuala Lumpur, the big capital city of Malaysia – 5 years as a medical student in the University of Malaya Medical Faculty, and 1 year as a houseman at the University Hospital, now known as University of Malaya Medical Centre (UMMC).

A DREAM REALISED

Established in 1962, the Faculty of Medicine, University of Malaya or UM Medical School is one of the thirteen faculties of the University of Malaya. I was part of its 9th batch of students. This was the first and the top medical school in Malaysia, with a very good reputation and ranking worldwide at the time.

I started my career in medicine in July 1972, as an undergraduate student. This was a 5-year course followed by a 1-year housemanship. The childhood ambition of my life finally came true like a dream realised! As far as I could remember, I had always wanted to be a medical doctor.

It was my sincere conviction becoming a medical doctor would give me a stable career – a better quality of life, and hopefully a stable source of income.

I would then be able to help people who are sick, render assistance, relieve pain, relieve suffering, relieve anxieties, and so on. My opportunity to do all these had finally arrived, thanks be to God, who always had my interest at heart and always had me covered.

RESIDENTIAL COLLEGE YEARS

For the first two years, I stayed in a residential college called the 1st College as this was the nearest college to the Faculty of Medicine. It was just a 30-minutes' walk up a long and winding road, but traveling by motorbike would only take 10 minutes. After a week's orientation, we were ready to attend classes.

On the first day of class, the Dean of Medicine, the late Emeritus Professor T.J. Danaraj (Prof. TJD) addressed the class of 72-77 in the grand clinical auditorium. I can still remember clearly the first words he spoke as though it was only yesterday. "Medicine is a lifelong course. It is never 5 years in a medical school". He went on to say that what we learn would be obsolete the moment we graduate. He was spot on regarding this and on retrospection, this turned out to be true.

The food at 1st College was horrible. The same food was being served every day and I could predict exactly what food will be served on a given day. Fortunately, there was a Chinese makan (food) shop in the college where I could go and buy Chinese fried noodles whenever I wanted to.

PROFESSOR DANARAJ

The late Professor Danaraj said that a doctor should never stop learning because medical knowledge progresses rapidly. Doctors owe it to their patients to keep up to date with new knowledge and new skills so as to be able to practice safely.

He said, a doctor is like a pilot. If a pilot stops flying and did not clock in the required number of flying hours, he would be grounded. I also remember the late Prof. TJD saying, "If you want to make plenty of money please go and do another course right now". By today's reckoning, this may not be so true because medical practice has become so commercialised and profit oriented. Today, doctors make a lot of money if they are famous and in the right specialty. Medicine actually is both a calling and a passion. Without these two key ingredients, it would be very difficult to pursue this career.

The late Prof. TJD was very knowledgeable but also very strict. He was a highly respected clinician and academician not only in Malaysia but also worldwide. We were very blessed to be taught by him. He was a very humble man. He set high standards for everyone to follow. Although he appeared to be very fierce in the classroom, he was actually very kind at heart, friendly, approachable, and helpful outside the classroom.

MENTORED BY THE BEST

The medical school curriculum was divided into 2 modules. The first being the preclinical module where the basic sciences such as anatomy, physiology, biochemistry, parasitology, pathology, clinical pharmacology, public health, statistics and so on were taught.

This was for a duration of two years. The second was the clinical module where students were allowed to clerk patients in the wards, to learn the art and science of medical practice through the teachings of the lecturers and professors – for three years.

The preclinical years were quite boring as we had to study a lot of basic sciences and were not allowed to interact with patients in the hospital. It seemed almost irrelevant at the time, but this was not true. Without the basic prerequisite knowledge to back us up, interacting with patients would be futile and even dangerous.

The pre-clinical years laid the strong basic foundation needed to understand and practice the art and science of medicine. After "surviving" the first 2 years, I moved on to the next 3 years of the clinical module.

Our batch consisting of 128 students was among the elite of Malaysian medical students at that time. We were truly blessed to have world renowned and eminent clinicians like the late Prof. TJD and others of his caliber to teach us the art, science and skill of medicine.

The late Prof. TJD told us not to refer to any patient as Case 1, Case 2, and so forth. Behind every case is a person, a human being with a name, and a soul. They were not to be called case number but to be addressed with dignity as individuals. He constantly inculcated within us that knowledge, honesty, ethics, empathy, compassion, kindness, right attitude, and good bedside manners were the basic ingredients to success.

I remember the clinical case conferences taught by the late Prof. TJD in the clinical auditorium. One student would be selected to present a case to the class in front of him. There would be tension in the room as the poor student at centre stage presented the case, terrified, expecting to be scolded and torn apart by the barrage of questions that followed.

Even those who did not present the case would be equally terrified, especially those sitting on the front rows, expecting to be hauled up by the learned Professor at any time. Even those who kept quiet could be hauled up for keeping quiet and not asking intelligent questions!

Then there were the teaching bedside ward rounds with late Prof. TJD. Ever so often, he would make a spot diagnosis just by looking at the patient – without even taking a history or doing a physical examination.

Students were amazed and spellbound. He would make spot diagnoses of patients with hyperthyroidism, hypothyroidism, end-stage renal failure, Parkinson's disease, rheumatoid arthritis, Paget's disease, mongolism, chorea athetosis, and so forth.

Prof. TJD taught us the importance of observation even as the patient walks into the room. He taught us how to use all our 5 senses of observing, hearing, smelling, touching, and feeling to make a diagnosis. A good history and a good physical examination is also the key to making a correct diagnosis.

I remember on one particular bedside teaching ward-round, where a patient with Chronic Rheumatic Heart Disease (CRHD) was presented to the late Prof. TJD. Palpating the character of the pulse, observing the JVP waveform, palpating for pitting edema, locating the position of the apex beat, palpating the precordium for thrills, and palpating the liver size was sufficient for him to arrive at the diagnosis.

He said that auscultation using the stethoscope was only required to confirm the diagnosis. The clinical acumen of the late Prof. TJD was hard to match. Besides cardiology, he also was a neurologist par excellence. I was very amazed by his ability to elicit clinical signs in neurology.

Medicine is both an art and a science. They say you can train a monkey to be an engineer, but you cannot train a monkey to be a doctor. A monkey could be trained in the science of medicine but not on the art of medicine which involved emotions, empathy, compassion, kindness, ethics and so on.

A MEDICAL STUDENT'S LIFE

My life as a medical student was not very dramatic or colourful by any stretch of the imagination. The preclinical years were very demanding. There were lectures to attend, practical work to do in the biochemistry laboratory, and practical work at the anatomy dissection room.

The class was divided into small groups for anatomy classes and each group was assigned one cadaver. Seeing a cadaver for the first time was not so frightening after all. Certainly not the way that was being portrayed to us in soap operas like Dr Quincy, etc. The cadaver had been preserved with some kind of embalming fluids to prevent decomposition. The smell of embalming fluids in the anatomy room was very strong and irritating to the eyes.

I remember the professor of anatomy telling us to respect the cadavers because they were there for us to learn anatomy. After every dissection, the cadaver gets smaller and smaller until there would be nothing left. Each group became closely knitted together and built up a relationship over the year.

ENCOUNTERING JESUS VIA THE VCF

We had a Christian fellowship group in my class, consisting of 12 Christian classmates who were Christians before they entered medical school. Although I was a free thinker, they invited me to join them in their weekly lunch fellowship meetings and other activities. They shared the gospel with me, gave me a Christian book to take home, and even prayed for me.

In my last spring cleaning, I came across this particular book with autographs and a lovely message. I became very emotional and could not hold back my tears reminiscing the divine connections God has brought along my path. My Christian friends were very helpful, reliable, honest, respectful, and good role models. Through their influence, I came to know about the Christian faith.

I also got to join the activities of the Varsity Christian Fellowship (VCF) and made friends with some of my seniors who were Christians and members of VCF. Then in 1976, on the 4th year of my study, I became a Christian through the sharing of one VCF member who visited me in my room when I was right in the middle of a personal crisis.

I was particularly fond of one classmate. He was a top scholar from Sarawak and had long beard. His nickname was "janggut', which means beard in Bahasa Malaysia.

We were of the same wavelength and frequency and got along very well. He was a good role model too and we spent quality time and did many things together in our free time. Unfortunately, he had a girlfriend in the later years and did not spend much time with me after that.

RECONNECTION

The student whom I taught tuition in Telok Intan entered University of Malaya in 1974 as a dentistry undergraduate. The faculty of Dentistry and Medicine was close by and we could meet easily. She also stayed in the 1st Residential College. We got along very well and rekindled our friendship. She was also a Perak State Scholarship holder.

CONCLUDING MY CLINICAL YEARS

For the last 3 clinical years, I moved to the Clinical Student Hostel (CSH), which was within walking distance from the medical school and the University Hospital. This was very much nearer than the 1st residential college.

College life in the CSH was interesting. Students were very naughty. I also remember a particular incident when the college warden's car was splashed with red paint. He must have offended some student who took the law into his own hands as an act of retaliation.

Students played volleyball, tennis, ping pong, and speak-takraw in the evening. Some of my classmates played mahjong late into the night even during examinations but still ended up with distinctions and placed amongst top of the class.

During lectures, they liked to sit on the back row of the lecture hall wearing dark-tinted spectacles. Some of my classmates were very rich and drove new BMWs while most of our Professors were driving older Volvos or Peugeots.

BUT BY THE GRACE OF GOD

I was not a very good student and hence, I found the medical course rather challenging. There were plenty of things to read, remember, memorize, conceptualize, and understand. By the grace of God, I managed to pass all my examinations and graduated with MBBS (Malaya) in 1977.

In those days, due to a shortage of doctors, medical graduates were required to start housemanship immediately after passing the final year examination. But to negotiate for a pay increase, our class refused to start housemanship immediately.

This initiative forced the government to increase the housemanship salary from RM650 to RM825. This was subsequently revised to RM1165.

After 12 months of housemanship in the University Hospital, Kuala Lumpur, I was finally registered with the Malaysian Medical

Council with a license to practice medicine in Malaysia. Some people called this a license to kill, but don't ever believe this! Life is sacred. The Hippocratic oath says, "Above all, do no harm".

After graduation, the MU Class of 72-77 still keep in touch and meet regularly to this day – through Facebook, WhatsApp and Class Reunions. Initially, we had Class Reunions once every 5 years but for the last 5 years, this has become a yearly affair. The last annual reunion was held successfully in Singapore, hosted by our Singapore classmates.

A reunion was planned to be held in Ipoh in 2020 but unfortunately, this event had to be canceled due to the COVID-19 pandemic. We hope that with the availability of the vaccine, this pandemic will be over sooner rather than later so we can all reconnect once again!

results

THE following candidates have passed their second year MBBS examination at the University of Malaya.

Abdul Munaff Gaffoor, Abdul Rahim bin Abdul Majid, Abdul Samad Sakijan, Abdullah Haron, Alias bin Dahalan, Aminah Abdul Rahman, Miss Ang Kim Tong, Bibyah Long Bidin, Chan Chee Wah, Chan Cheng Kuen.

Chan Weng Chew, Che Lima Che Ismail, Chew Kok Wah, Chan Sung [illegible], Chia Hong Soong, Chin Cheok Ngee, Miss Chew Sun Yan, Miss D'Cruz Pamela, Dominic Sungam, Foo Lai Sin, Miss Gan Eng Meng, Goh Boon Huat, Goon Hong Koui, Cunasagran Ramasamy, Ha Tong Swee, Francis Halil Rahman, Hamidah Ismail, Hamzah bin Musa, Harun bin Ibrahim.

Hersary M. Mohd Noor, Hon Peck Lim, Khaw Chin Hooi, Kooy Tong Hin, Koh Chan Sing, Koh Mia Tuang, Koh Tat Seng, Miss Kong [illegible] Ling, Law Leak Kei.

Lee Ah Hoe, Lee Pin Chiang, Lee Khim Khoon, Miss Lee Kim Kee, Lee Siew Sun (distinction in Medical Microbiology), Lee Tong Weng.

Leong Shawn Chong (distinction in Parasitology), Liding Anak Juhyan, Miss Lim Beng Hoon (distinction in Medical Microbiology), Lim Chin Theam, Low Seang Gip, Madhukar Chunilal.

Mahinder Singh, Mashah bin Omar, Mastura bt. Mohamed, Mohamad Padzil bin Man, Mohamad Hashim bin Nik Omar, Mohammad bin [illegible] [illegible] [illegible]

Siew Lee Ping, Siti Radha bt. Jamal, Suraiya Banu Hussein.

Suzani Yahya, Syed Mansur Syed Ahmad Almashoor, Miss Tan Beng Hoon, Miss Tan Seok Kheng, Miss Teh Siok Khoi, Miss Ting Siew Ong, Miss Toh Sew Hoot, Miss Tong Wai Sin, Wan Ali bin Tuanku Haji Madah, Wong Chee Sing (distinctions in Medical Microbiology and Pathology), Miss Wong Chew Lan, Miss Wong Mee Lian, Miss Wong Mei Cham.

Peter Wong Toh Lee, Miss Wong Yoke Meng, Miss Wu Loo Ling, Yap Ngim Looke (distinction in Parasitology), Yong Kam Leng, Yong Kim Shong, Yung Ying Pah, Zainon Ahmad Abdul Kareem.

The following candidates have been awarded provisional passes:

Abang Yusup Abang Haji Rasak, Abdullah Salleh, Aida Bustafa bt. Mohammad Ghazali, Chee Lai Tong, Haru Rahmah, Jee Chiew Sum, Juraidah bt. Ahmad, Miss Lim Siew Khin, Mahmud Ahmad Mansur, Mohamad Ramli bin Hj. Mohamad Kari, Muhammad Ali Noor bin Abdul Ghani, Nik Hishamudin bin Hashim, Othman Ahmad, Miss Rosiinah bt. Mohamad, Swaminathan Manickam, Wong Hua Seh, Zainal bin Wan.

☆

THE following candidates have passed their first year BDS examination. (Distinctions for subjects in brackets).

Abdul Aziz b. Abdul Hamid, Ahmad Bahrain, Othman, B. K. Mohanan, Baru Langub, Chan Siew Lian, Chia Sei [illegible]

2nd Year MBBS Results – My name (Koh Chan Sing) is on the third paragraph. Photo courtesy of Dr. Koh Mia Tuang

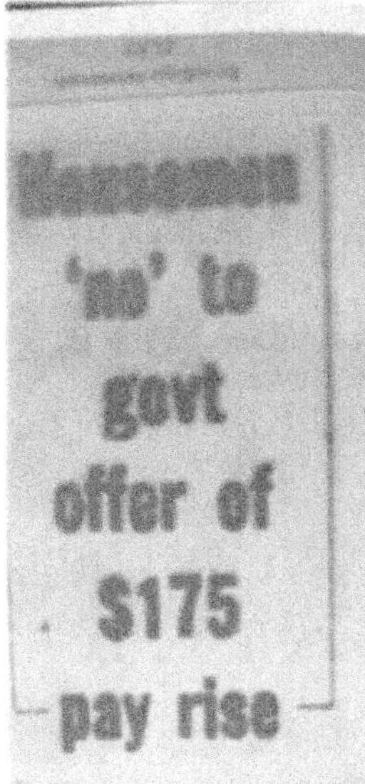

Housemen 'no' to govt offer of $175 pay rise

KUALA LUMPUR, Sat. — Housemen have decided not to accept the government's offer of an allowance of $825—an increase of $175.

A spokesman for the Union of Malaysian Housemen said today they still felt their case for an increase to $1,105 was justified.

"We have not received an increase in our allowance for 15 years whereas other government servants have had two salary revisions."

The decision to reject the government's offer was taken at an emergency meeting last night of housemen and medical students representatives.

Not trainees

... Act 1971, Section 13 Clause Two, housemen should be considered employees of the government and not trainees.

"Therefore, they should be entitled for a salary and not an allowance, and the period of housemanship should be recognised as a year of government service.

"We would like to point out that nowhere in the Act does it state that we are undergoing a period of training."

The spokesman said they were in fact "engaged in employment in a resident medical capacity."

New scheme

The spokesman said they would seek a dialogue with Deputy Prime Minister Dr. Mahathir Mohamad, who is also chairman of the Cabinet committee on the new pay scheme, at the earliest possible opportunity.

A total of 119 University of Malaya medical students, who passed their final year examination recently, decided last Wednesday not to seek registration with the Malaysian Medical Council because they were not happy with the pay and conditions of service for housemen.

They have decided not to serve the government until their grievances were settled.

Newspaper Clip of the Housemen's negotiation for an allowance raise. Photo courtesy of Dr. Lee Aik Hoe

THIS WORLD IS NOT OUR HOME

This world is not our home,
We are just passing through,
Whatever good that we can do,
Now is the time to do.

We bring nothing when we come,
We take nothing when we go,
Godliness with contentment is the way to go.

Whatever is noble, whatever is true,
Whatever is lovely, whatever is good,
This we will do.

Whatever is praiseworthy, whatever is pure,
Meditate more and more.

CHAPTER FOUR

HOUSEMANSHIP IN THE *IVORY TOWER*

"I have sometimes sat alone here of an evening, listening, until I have made the echoes out to be the echoes of all the footsteps that are coming by and by into our lives."

- *A Tale of Two Cities, Charles Dickens.*

In July 1977, I found myself working in the ivory tower called the University Hospital Kuala Lumpur, presently known as the University of Malaya Medical Centre (UMMC), as an intern, or houseman.

This was a one-year compulsory training for all new medical graduates before being granted full registration as medical practitioners under the Malaysian Medical Council. I spent the first 6 months of internship in Internal Medicine and the second 6 months in Obstetrics and Gynecology.

HOUSEMANSHIP

I was provided free accommodation in the houseman's quarters located on the 14th floor (which was the top floor) of the University Hospital block. This was both convenient and essential as I had been assigned to the on-call ward and could access it easily from here when I was needed.

Accommodation was very basic but adequate for me. My financials started from scratch. I only had one hundred ringgit in my bank account when I started housemanship. Truly this was "the best of times, and it was the worst of times".

As a medical student, I could only afford a motorbike. So whenever it rained, I got all wet. Riding a motorcycle was also very dangerous in the event of an accident. So with my houseman's salary, I sold my motorbike and bought my first car for RM1,000.00 – an old second-hand Renault model.

However, it gave me lots of mechanical problems and needed regular repairs. So after a few months, I sold it off and bought a 2-door Toyota Corolla sedan for RM4,000.00. This car served me very faithfully and did not break down at all.

INTERNAL MEDICINE

I will start my story with Internal Medicine first. Each house officer was assigned to one medical ward. I was assigned to ward 13, located on the 13th floor. I took care of 28 patients. This ward was under the care of a medical officer, a lecturer, and a Professor. As a houseman, I was required to know all my patients. The medical officer, lecturer, and professor walked in and out of the ward, but I was there all the time.

I worked from 8 am until late in the evening but I had to be back at midnight to look after the cases in ward 13. I did not take a liking to this "Cinderella Call" because I could not go anywhere after midnight. My freedom was restricted, but on retrospect, this was good training.

It drove home the point to me that life as a doctor was not going to be easy. I need to have the calling, the passion, the commitment, and the willingness to sacrifice my time wholeheartedly. This certainly was not a profession for those with half-hearted commitment.

Housemanship in Medicine was an extremely demanding job. My typical day started with an early breakfast in the hospital canteen. Then it was off to the ward to do a fast round, making sure that I knew each patient by name, provisional diagnosis, latest blood tests and imaging results, management plans, and so forth.

I had to familiarize myself with any new admissions that might have come in the night before. By 10 am, the medical officer would come with the lecturer to do the daily ward rounds.

Going from one patient to the next until the last one may take a couple of hours, depending on the complexities of each patient. After that, I had to clerk all the new cases admitted via the outpatient department or the accident and emergency department. My job was to take a full history, do a physical examination, and document these on to the case notes.

The medical officer would come by later to check on each case and order the appropriate investigations and recommend the plan of management. Then it was back to clerking new cases, doing ward procedures, reviewing tests reports, and so forth until 5 pm or later before passing the reins over to the next houseman on call.

The highlight of my stint in Medicine was the weekly Professorial grand teaching ward round. My Professor will come in at 9 am with the medical officer, and my job was to present every case to her from head to toe. The ward round usually took a long time to complete because the Professor was very long-winded with her teaching. She frequently sidetracked by telling us other unrelated stories, but no one dared to interrupt her!

By lunchtime, we would have covered possibly 8 or 10 patients at the most and there were so many more to cover! The team adjourned for a quick lunch break and resumed the grand rounds until 3 or 4 pm. After this, I was back to clerking new cases and reviewing reports. By this time there would be a backlog of cases to clerk and my day would end very late!

One day, a very prominent and famous radio Disc Jockey was admitted into ward 13. She used to come on air every night on national radio from 11 pm until midnight with her selection of sentimental songs.

She was a client and good friend of my Professor and I had to give her special treatment. Her voice was so sweet and soothing. Listening to her speak in person was just like listening to her on national radio every night.

The housemanship provided me with hands-on experience, learning through apprenticeship, supervision and bedside teaching. The medical officer was my mentor and I tagged along with him as close as I could without encroaching too much onto his personal space. Now was the time to put into practice all that I had learned in the last 5 years of medical school.

I could be diligent and learn as much as possible or choose to be slipshod and just do the bare minimum. It was entirely up to me and I chose the former route.

I got on very well with the nursing sisters, building up a good relationship with them over time. I learned a lot from them as some of them had been in their profession for decades. I also learned a lot from the medical officer, lecturer, and Professor.

OBSTETRICS AND GYNAECOLOGY

After completing the first 6 months in Internal Medicine, I moved to Obstetrics and Gynaecology for the second 6 months. The stint in Obstetrics and Gynaecology was an entirely different ball game There was no more "Cinderella Call".

If I was not on call, I would be free after doing all the duties for the day and passing the reins over to the next houseman on call. History taking was short, sweet, and straight to the point. Lecturers and Professors did not breathe down my neck and were not interested in a detailed history of every case.

Here I learned how to deliver babies, assisted in forceps and vacuum deliveries, assisted in Caesarean Sections, tubal ligation, vasectomy, and other minor surgeries. I could recollect some dramatic, sad, and humorous incidents as well.

A Malay lady who worked in the department of Obstetrics and Gynecology as a clerk came in for a Caesarean Section and died suddenly the following day. The lecturer said she had a fat embolism, a rare but fatal clinical syndrome.

One day, when I was on call, a lady who came in for an emergency hysterectomy had a postoperative intractable massive hemorrhage. The Professor on call was called into the operation theatre. To stop the bleeding he performed bilateral internal iliac artery ligation and arrested the bleeding.

Many pints of blood were transfused but she survived! The Professor was praised for his prompt and life-saving decision. This was the first time bilateral internal iliac artery ligation was done for post-hysterectomy hemorrhage in the University Hospital.

Of course, the most unforgettable, most painful, and most unfortunate incident was the fatal MH 653 air-crash on 4th December 1977 which took the life of the late Professor I.S. Puvan, Professor of Obstetrics and Gynaecology of University Hospital, plus 7 members of the aircrew, and 92 other passengers on board. He was a Professor with a big heart, impeccable bedside manners, powerful persona and was well loved by doctors, staffs, and patients.

I miss him dearly even up to this day. I recall working in the labour ward one night when he came in and give RM 20 to one of the midwives to buy supper for everyone on duty. In those days, RM 20 was a large sum of money.

According to the Bureau of Labor Statistics consumer price index of the year 2020, RM 20 in 1977 is equivalent to RM 86 in 2020. His impeccable bedside manners and pleasant personality were second to none and hard to match. He was the Malaysian equivalent of the television persona Dr. Kildare.

Working in the labour ward was both equally exciting and dramatic. We could not predict when patients would come in for labour. They usually came in at the oddest hours of the night but seldom during office hours.

Patients came in with variable degrees of pain. Some came in screaming and shouting while others came in with more manageable and tolerable pain. It had to do with the respective patients' pain threshold.

Generally speaking, Indian women seem to have a much lower pain threshold than women of other ethnicity. They tend to scream and shout with each contraction and demand more and more pethidine for pain relief which is not good for the fetus.

I learned a lot from the midwives. Some of them had been in the profession for decades and were very experienced. The Indian word for breathing in and out is "muchu" and the Indian word for pushing with all of your life is "mukku". When you want the patient to breathe in and out, you would say "muchu" and when you want her to push with all of her life you would say "mukku".

The problem was when the houseman mixed up these two commands and said push with all your life when he wanted her to breathe in and out…and to say breathe in and out when he wanted her to push with all her life!

I was told that this had happened to some houseman before my stint but whether this was true or not, I cannot confirm. But then again, as they say, "truth is stranger than fiction". Sometimes the truth out there is more bizarre than our imagination.

I remember reporting for duty one day in the labour ward, after taking over from the previous houseman. The ward seemed to be too quiet because there was no patient in labour. All the midwives were relaxing, having a jolly good time, and you could have heard a pin drop.

Being a newbie to the trade, I blurted out the question, "Why is there no patient in labour?" The mid-wives rebuked me, saying that I had jinxed them with my question. Not long after this, patients started arriving – one after another, non-stop until my shift was over! An interesting lesson this one was for me that "Silence is Golden" – as the saying goes.

MARRIAGE

On 31st August 1977, I married my wife who was then a final year student in Dentistry in the University of Malaya. Upon marriage, we stayed together in the houseman's quarters.

As good as it gets – we got married on 31st August 1977

TIME

One year, 365 days went by,
365 opportunities set aside,
One month, 30 days came and went,
30 opportunities to connect with friends.

One week, 7 days of good, clean fun,
7 opportunities to save enough,
One day, 24 hours to talk with someone,
24 opportunities to walk as one.

One hour, 60 minutes to touch someone,
60 opportunities to share heart to heart,
One minute, 60 seconds to share WhatsApp,
60 opportunities to be a friend.

CHAPTER

FIVE

TAIPING TO *LABUAN*

"Nothing that we do, is done in vain. I believe, with all my soul, that we shall see triumph."

- A Tale of Two Cities, Charles Dickens.

After completing my housemanship in the Ivory Tower of University Hospital, I joined the Ministry of Health

Malaysia (MOH) in the middle of 1978.

My first posting was to Taiping District Hospital as a medical officer. This is a small hospital with very basic disciplines such as Medicine, General Surgery, Obstetrics and Gynaecology, Orthopedic Surgery, Dentistry, Oral Surgery, and Anaesthesiology.

MY TAIPING EXPERIENCE

Taiping is the second largest town in Perak with a thriving population of 245,182 in 2013. Located 48km north of Ipoh and 78km south of George Town, Penang, Taiping is famous for its Taiping Zoo and Night Safari, Taiping Lake Gardens, and Maxwell Hill. My wife also followed me and was also posted to Taiping Hospital as a government dental surgeon.

Working in Taiping was an entirely different ball game compared to working in the University Hospital – which was a teaching hospital. The Taiping District Hospital was a service orientated hospital and thus there was no emphasis on training, research, or continuous medical education.

In those days, there was a shortage of doctors and the patient load was heavy. The hospital had a vacancy for 15 medical officers but at any one time, there would only be about 5 medical officers in the establishment. This is in stark contrast to the situation today where there are way too many doctors.

The medical library facilities in Taiping were severely inadequate and the system was not at all conducive for any postgraduate medical education or research. Fortunately, the consultant Physician at that time was very academic-minded and had a passion for teaching. He conducted evening classes to teach medical officers how to pass the MRCP (U.K.) Part 1 exams.

This was Part 1 of the Internal Medicine Specialist Examination of the United Kingdom. All the medical officers who were preparing for this examination benefitted from his teaching, including me.

OUTPATIENT DEPARTMENT

For the first 6 months, I was posted to the outpatient department. The patient load was very heavy. On a typical day I had to see close to 100 patients – and it was just way too much! I did not have sufficient time to take a proper patient history and conduct a thorough physical examination. We only had 2 medical officers manning the outpatient department whereas we should have had at least 4 to cope with our patient load.

The government was terribly short of medical doctors and could not fill the vacancies. Fast forward to the year 2020, where we now have a glut of medical doctors in the market. The oversupply today is such that new medical graduates have to wait for a year or so before they can start housemanship!

During my time, we started housemanship immediately after passing our final year examination. Compulsory service in government medical institutions have been abolished today. In my time we had to do 2-year compulsory government service. Medical officers today are employed on contract basis. In my time, we were employed as permanent staff. How the times have changed!

MOBILE HEALTH CLINIC

After 6 months at the outpatient department, I was posted to the mobile health clinic team. The mobile health clinic team consisted of one medical officer, one hospital assistant, one staff nurse, one dispenser, one attendant, and one driver. The mobile health clinic offered outpatient services 5 days a week, from Monday to Friday. On Saturdays, we rested.

The mobile clinic van travelled from Taiping Hospital to the rural towns in the Larut, Matang, and Selama district. Upon arriving at the site, we treated the public using the van as a mobile clinic. Our van was stocked up with clinic appointment cards, case sheets, medication, syringes, needles and other things needed to run the clinic.

We offered consultation and treatment for simple, stable conditions and dispensed basic medication for hypertension, diabetes, antibiotics, deworming, creams, lotions, eye drops, and so forth. Patients requiring hospitalisation or specialist care were referred to the Taiping Hospital via a referral letter.

Our team left Taiping Hospital as early as 7.30 am and returned to base by 4 pm daily on clinic days. In exchange for our services, some satisfied patients gave us fish, crabs, prawns, fruits, and vegetables to take home as tokens of appreciation.

Besides medical practice, my wife and I also attended the Taiping Gospel Hall church for Sunday services and weekly Bible studies. We stayed in a rented house which was about 30-minutes' drive from the Taiping hospital. My parents also moved-in to stay with us in Taiping.

MINDEF & MY YEARS IN LABUAN

After a year in Taiping, I joined the Ministry of Defence (MINDEF) as an army medical officer on a 2-year contract. The government of Malaysia drafted me into the army to serve in the Ministry of Defence for 2 years.

I had to undergo a 1-month army training course at Kinrara Camp in Kuala Lumpur after which I was commissioned as an army officer with the rank of a Captain. After the commissioning, I was posted to serve at an army hospital in the Royal Malaysian Airforce Base (RMAF) in Labuan, East Malaysia for 2 years.

So towards the end of 1979, my wife and I left on an army aircraft, a Charlie 130, from Kuala Lumpur en route to Labuan, to report for my first tour of duty. The flight took us three and a half hours before we touched down at the RMAF Airbase in Labuan.

We were provided with free accommodation in the officers' quarters near the military hospital. My wife was also posted to Labuan District Hospital as a dental surgeon.

LABUAN RMAF MILITARY HOSPITAL

The military hospital in RMAF airbase Labuan was a small setup with a facility for outpatient consultation and a treatment room for minor surgical procedures. My job was to look after the healthcare needs of all the army officers, rank and file soldiers, air-force officers, airmen, and their family members.

I also carried out yearly medical examinations for all the soldiers as part of their service requirement. Patients who required admission or major surgery would be referred to the Labuan District Hospital nearby.

The clinical workload was very light. I only got to see about 10 patients daily. In the evening, I played tennis, and at night I used to visit the officers' mess for social gatherings, chit-chat, and refreshments. The beer in the mess was particularly cheap as it was a duty-free item.

Life in the army was very relaxing. Clinical work was minimal, and this gave me a lot of time to study for the MRCP (U.K.) Part 1 Examination, (Internal Medicine Specialist Examination) which I successfully passed before concluding my tour of duty.

As a Captain, I had to wear an army uniform at work. Thus, I would be saluted and called "sir" many times a day by the rank and file, and I had to salute back as a sign of courtesy. Conversely, if I were to bump into any senior officer, I had to salute him and address him as "sir" and he in turn would salute me.

In the armed forces discipline was of utmost importance. I was told that in the event of a war, the discipline of one's soldiers could very well determine whether they lived or died.

LABUAN DISTRICT HOSPITAL

Since work in the army was light, I volunteered my service in the government Labuan District Hospital. The medical officer in the Labuan Hospital was my friend and he allowed me to work with him.

He was quite a good clinician and surgeon, who was able to do appendectomy, hernia repair, conduct delivery, caesarean section, and so on. In those days, there was no anaesthetist. The hospital assistant would administer the general anesthesia even though he was not an anesthetist.

A COUPLE OF TRAGEDIES IN LABUAN

They say life is short. I had a businessman friend in Labuan with whose family my wife and I were very close. It was very heart wrenching when he committed suicide by hanging due to business failure and inability to settle debts.

In another unfortunate incident, I lost one of my pilot friends who was in his thirties when his helicopter crashed in bad weather during a search and rescue mission. He left behind a devastated young wife and an infant. This incident was particularly heart-wrenching and to this day, I still get quite emotional whenever I think about it.

IT'S ALL ABOUT WHO YOU KNOW

I got to know and made friends with senior air force officers, pilots, and their families. We used to invite other officers to our house for meals and fellowship. Sometimes, when I travelled in an army aircraft on official duty, the pilot would invite me to sit next to him in the cockpit.

Once when I was sitting in the cockpit, I saw a genuine full-circle rainbow. It was breathtaking, to say the least. The panoramic view from the cockpit was extremely impressive and beautiful, especially during take-off and landing. Even after my tour of duty I maintained contact with some of the air force officers in West Malaysia.

They say it is not what you know but *who you know.* One of my Bidor cousins was working as an airman in the Labuan RMAF airbase. One day, he told me that he had been applying for a scholarship for many years but had always been rejected and was not even shortlisted.

On hearing this, I approached his commanding officer, an air force pilot with the rank of Major. He said, "Oh I did not know that he is your cousin. You should have told me earlier!" Within three months, my cousin received a scholarship to study aeronautical engineering in the USA. Considering the fact that my cousin had waited several years with no results, that was truly amazing – a "wow" moment!

IT'S A SMALL WORLD AFTER ALL

They say that the world is a small place. One day in Labuan, I bumped into someone who said he recognized me but could not exactly place where he knew me from.

As we continued our chit-chat, I found out that he used to be my MES scout master in Tanjong Malim. He was now working in the Royal Malaysian Navy Base in Labuan as an Admiral, a senior Royal Malaysian Navy officer. The world is indeed small, and you could bump into someone you know in the most unexpected of places!

On the spiritual development front, my wife and I also attended an Anglican Church in Labuan for weekly Sunday services, bible study, and other activities.

A TRULY VALUABLE EXPERIENCE

Serving in the army was a valuable experience, away from the hustle and bustle of city life. This unforgettable tour of duty was second to none. The highlight of my army life was the annual regimental night held in the officer's mess. All officers arrived in style, dressed in their official regimental attire. Sitting would be according to ranks. A multiple course meal was served according to protocol and all the officers had to adhere strictly to it.

We had to know how to use different kinds of knives, forks, and spoons for the different courses and correctly hold them. It was a solemn affair, with speeches, toasts, and so forth. No one would be allowed to leavc until the commanding officer left. Fortunately, they gave us a rehearsal on training of cutlery usage and other protocols before the regimental night, otherwise it would have been disastrous!

LABUAN'S DUTY-FREE PERKS

Labuan is an Island located off the coast of Sabah. At that time, it was a tax-free port. Electronic and electrical products were far cheaper in Labuan. Imported cars were also very cheap as these were completely duty-free.

Almost all army and air force officers drove flashy and expensive cars, waiting to ship them back to West Malaysia at the end of their tour of duty. I bought a Honda Accord, and my wife bought a Nissan 120Y at a fraction of the cost in West Malaysia. We sent our cars back to West Malaysia via a Navy ship at the end of my tour of duty.

A TIME FOR EVERYTHING

A time for everything,
A time for every activity under heavens,
A time to be born, a time to die,
A time to plant, a time to uproot,
A time to kill, a time to heal,
A time to tear down, a time to build.

A time to weep, a time to laugh,
A time to mourn, a time to dance,
A time to scatter stones, a time to gather them,
A time to embrace, a time to refrain from
embracing.

A time to search, a time to give up,
A time to keep, a time to throw away,
A time to tear, a time to mend.

A time to be silent, a time to speak,
A time to love, a time to hate,
A time for war, a time for peace.
Ecclesiastes 3:1-8

CHAPTER SIX

IVORY TOWER, LONDON, *& TELOK INTAN*

"He knew enough of the world to know that there is nothing in it better than the faithful service of the heart."

- A Tale of Two Cities, Charles Dickens.

In 1981, after completing my tour of duty with the armed forces in Labuan, I hung up my "Captain" title and returned to a civilian life working in University Hospital Kuala Lumpur as a medical officer on contract for 2 years. I joined the Department of Internal Medicine.

By this time, after 3 years of "honeymoon" away from academic medicine, I was quite rusty and outdated. It took me a little while to get back into the rhythm once again but with proper guidance and a suitable environment, everything fell into place once more.

EXPANDING MY HORIZONS

Working in a teaching hospital was a prerequisite for postgraduate training and accreditation in Internal Medicine. The medical library here was fully equipped.

Here I had the privilege to see a large variety of cases, the opportunity for case presentations, research, and even publish articles in local, regional, and international peer-reviewed medical journals. I was interested in Cardiology and Neurology, and was very close to the Professors of Cardiology and Neurology. I was their blue-eyed boy, so to speak.

Meanwhile, my wife was posted to a government dental clinic in Jalan Bangsar, Kuala Lumpur. We stayed in a rented a house in Taman Seputeh. During this time, our first son was born in the University Hospital. My parents came to live with us to help look after our son.

Besides medical practice, we attended the First Baptist Church in Taman Jaya, Petaling Jaya. The senior pastor then was a very godly man who gave great life-changing sermons with altar calls every Sunday.

ENTER LONDON

After 2 years in the University Hospital, I left Kuala Lumpur for London to sit for my MRCP (U.K.) Part 2 (Internal Medicine Specialist Examination). I was attached to St. Giles Hospital as a locum Senior House Officer with accommodation provided in the hospital. This gave me a source of income but the taxation rate in the UK was very high.

Nevertheless, this allowed me the opportunity to acclimatize and be exposed to different clinical practice scenarios in the United Kingdom, which was quite different from Malaysia. On weekends, I used to visit a relative who lived in London. I also took the opportunity to visit all the different tourist attractions in and around London and also made day trips organized by the hospital staff to a border town in France.

EXPERIENCING ROMANS 8:28

The MRCP Part 2 examination was divided into two parts –

the theory module, and the practical module which were held several weeks apart. A candidate had to pass the theory module first before he was allowed to proceed to the practical module. Unfortunately, at that time, there was a trade war between the Malaysian and the British governments.

Malaysia had just instituted the buy British last policy. Due to this, the failure rates among Malaysian candidates sitting for the MRCP, UK was much higher than usual. Thank God, I was able to make it through the theory module and practical module on my first attempt and was awarded the MRCK (UK) Diploma. God was working behind the scenes to help me through the circumstances of my life.

I claim the promise of God's Word in Romans 8:28, "*And we know that all things work together for good to those who love God, to those who are the called according to His purpose.*".

RETURN TO MALAYSIA

In 1983, after returning from London, I was posted to the General Hospital Kuala Lumpur as a Physician. Unfortunately, I was very unhappy in General Hospital Kuala Lumpur. I was bullied by the Senior Physician and other colleagues in the department of Medicine.

The Senior Physician seemed to have a racist tendency and found fault in everything that I did or try to do. Eventually, unable to tolerate the abuses any longer, I resigned from government service and started a private practice in a rural town called Kuala Kubu Bahru in Selangor. My wife also followed me by getting a job as a government dental surgeon in Kuala Kubu Bahru.

LIFE IN KKB

Life was more relaxed in Kuala Kubu Bahru or KKB, as it was a small rural town, on the foot of Fraser's Hill, away from the hustle and bustle of the big city Kuala Lumpur. I practiced as a general practitioner (GP) treating only outpatients.

We attended the Gospel Hall in Kuala Kubu Bahru. The pastor was a good friend of ours – someone whom we knew before reconnecting here in KKB. We attended his weekly Bible studies and weekly Sunday services. My wife and I were baptized in Gospel Hall in Kuala Kubu Bahru.

By now our second son was born and we were a family of four. My parents also moved in to live in with us to help look after the children. We lived in a rented house in KKB. My sons were very blessed to have their grandpa and grandma look after them. My parents loved their two grandsons very much.

BACK TO TELOK INTAN

In 1984, I moved from Kuala Kubu Bahru, KKB, to Telok Intan to work as a Physician in a Specialist Center with outpatient and inpatient facilities. My wife also followed me from KKB and worked in a government dental clinic in Telok Intan. Here we finally bought our first house in Telok Intan, which was within walking distance to the Specialist Center. My parents also moved over and lived with us in Telok Intan.

CONNECTION TO THE CHURCH

Everywhere we moved, we joined a local church where we

could serve, grow, and fellowship with the congregation. We worshiped in the Wesley Methodist Church in Telok Intan. The pastor was a very Godly man, who gave life-transforming sermons every Sunday. We regularly attended his weekly Sunday services and weekday Bible studies.

REDEDICATION TO CHRIST

In 1985, during the Christmas dinner organized by the Wesley Methodist Church, the pastor gave a message which spoke directly to my heart. After the message, he gave an altar call, invited those who wanted to rededicate their lives to Christ to come forward to be prayed for.

I responded to the altar call, went forward and the pastor prayed for me. Since then, my spiritual life was revived, and I began to have a thirst for more of God's presence in my life. I started to read and study the Bible on my own with great earnest and intensity.

In Wesley Methodist Church, I participated in the Navigator 2:7 Bible Study Series. This was a weekly Bible Study over 6 months. The highlight of this Bible Study was memorizing Bible verses. We were given a large number of Bible verses printed onto small cards. By repeating these verses many times a day and using the cards as memory aids, we could memorize all the verses. Even until today, I can still remember and recite these verses correctly.

THE CALEB GROUP & FGBMFI

With another group, I also started a weekly fasting and prayer meeting in my house. We called ourselves the Caleb group. We fasted breakfast and lunch before coming together for corporate worship and prayer at 7:30 pm.

At the end of the worship and prayer meeting, we break our fast and have dinner in my house. This went on for almost 1 year and after that we decided to stop. During this particular year, I saw so many breakthroughs in my life and in the church.

I was also active as a committee member of the Full Gospel Businessmen's Fellowship International Ipoh Chapter, FGBMFI. We organized weekly lunch meetings and monthly dinner meetings.

We invited non-Christian friends to listen to prominent Christian professionals sharing their evangelistic testimonies followed by lunch or dinner. Those who responded to the altar calls were directed to local churches for follow up and discipleship.

MY PARENTS – TRULY A BLESSING

We were blessed to have my parents live with us to look after the children when we were out working. Without them, it would have been impossible for us to cope.

We also had Indonesian maids to help out with domestic assistance. They were on contract for 2 years. Just when our children got used to one maid, the 2 years was up, and it was time for goodbyes. Our children were very close to their grandparents.

Both my parents became Christians through our influence. They have both passed on to be with the Lord Jesus due to old age. As much as I miss them, I know that one day we will all be reunited again in heaven.

My parents with my wife and sons

THE COVID GUY

2019 ended with a cry,
2020 full of surprise,
Chained to our homes by the Covid guy.

Economies collapsing left and right,
Hoteliers crying out with a sigh,

Food Panda laughing to the bank,
Grab Food flourishing with a bang!

Internet shoppers shopping in style,
2020 ended with another cry,
For 2021 to vaccinate the Covid guy.

CHAPTER SEVEN

MALAYSIA TO

NEW ZEALAND & BACK

"A wonderful fact to reflect upon, that every human creature is constituted to be that profound secret and mystery to every other."

- A Tale of Two Cities, Charles Dickens.

In 1986, I moved again from Telok Intan to join the Ipoh Specialist Center as a Physician. My family and parents joined me a few months later after I bought a house and settled down in Ipoh. Here, my third son was born at the Ipoh Specialist Centre.

JOSHUA'S CHALLENGING TIME IN IPOH

In Ipoh, my children studied at the Anglo Chinese School (ACS). My second son, Joshua encountered great difficulty in Standard 1. He was very shy, introverted, and withdrawn.

He often cried and refused to go to school. My late father had to accompany him every day to school. He even had to stay through recess time to buy Joshua food from the canteen – for he did not even know how to buy food.

To compound matters further, Joshua was bullied by a Punjabi student. His Standard 1 class teacher also complained about his progress. Fortunately one day, "big uncle" (my mother's elder brother) from Bidor came to the school to visit my late father.

It turned out that he knew Joshua's class teacher very well as she was also from Bidor. After big uncle had a talk with the class teacher, she showed special attention to Joshua and helped him, instead of criticising him.

Joshua was a loner and did not even have a single friend in class up to this point. But God was good to Joshua. One day, God sent one of his classmates to befriend him. They were inseparable from that day onwards. This boy taught Joshua how to conduct himself and interact with people, how to play football, etc.

Through the influence of this boy, Joshua slowly but surely overcame his introversion. I thank God for bringing this boy into Joshua's life. Till today, his parents are our family friends. However, there is a sad note here that this beloved classmate passed away in 2019 due to a fire accident in his office. May his soul rest in peace.

GROWING DEEPER IN GOD'S WORD

The pastor who was in Telok Intan was also transferred to the Wesley Methodist Church in Ipoh. To follow him, I joined that church too. There were more opportunities for Bible studies in Ipoh.

I attended Bible seminars taught by a very anointed Bible teacher who flew in from Singapore to Ipoh once every 6 weeks. I followed his teachings from the book of Genesis to the book of

Revelation. I took down notes and bought most of his audio tapes, CDs and books.

BROTHER PAUL TAN'S INFLUENCE

This anointed Bible teacher was the late Brother Paul Tan, who was once the Principal of Tung Ling Bible Seminary, Singapore. His late father was a co-worker of the late Watchman Nee. Paul was an excellent bible teacher who taught based on a verse-by-verse, grammatico-historical exegesis and exposition.

He taught me every book of the Bible starting from Genesis to Revelation, covering the whole counsel of God. He was able to truly "bring the Bible to life". I was inspired by his anointing, bible knowledge, communication skills, spiritual gifting, love for the Lord, and His Word.

Brother Paul was my friend, role model, and mentor. I was very sad when he was called home to the Lord. His influence inspired me to pursue fulltime studies in a Bible College later on.

TRAVERSING THE GLOBE FROM IPOH

Medical practice in Ipoh was more challenging. I had to manage inpatients and outpatients. To further my career development, I held short term fellowships at the Royal Northshore Hospital, Sydney, in 1989 and 1991 as a clinical fellow in Cardiology.

During my absence from Ipoh, I employed locums to do my duties for me. My job in Ipoh also allowed me to travel widely for medical seminars and conferences locally, regionally, and internationally. This was a blessing as I was able see so many countries around the world.

In 1994, Ipoh Specialist Centre, which was owned by group of specialists, was sold to the Johore Corporation through a corporate takeover. The new owner was very aggressive and subsequently listed the hospital together with Johore Specialist Centre as a public listed company called KPJ Healthcare.

Ipoh Specialist Centre was renamed KPJ Ipoh Specialist Hospital. The new owner turned the hospital around by transforming it into a billion-ringgit turnover business enterprise within 10 years.

Not long after the public listing, I left Ipoh Specialist Centre and set up my standalone Cardiology Specialist Clinic in Ipoh City Centre with facilities for Echocardiography, Treadmill Exercise Stress Testing and 24-hour Holter Monitoring. At the end of 1998, I sold my practice to another doctor and moved to Auckland, New Zealand with my whole family namely, my wife and three sons.

THE 1997 ASIAN FINANCIAL CRISIS

In private practice, I was able to afford more things as my earnings were significantly higher than in government service. In 1997, when the Asian financial crisis hit, Malaysia suffered a huge depreciation of the ringgit due to attacks by currency speculators and massive capital flight. Malaysia only managed to recover from this setback sometime in 1999.

Share prices dropped steeply and suddenly. Share market investors suffered heavy losses and some even went bankrupt overnight! Property prices dropped drastically, and cars were also sold at heavy discounts. Fortunately, I was not impacted badly and did not suffer any financial loss. Due to the financial meltdown, I was able to buy my house in Ipoh at a bargain price.

BIBLE COLLEGE OF NEW ZEALAND

In the year 2000, I studied in Laidlaw Bible College, previously known as Bible College of New Zealand, pursuing a 1-year Diploma of Graduate in Theology course. After my graduation, I continued with my Post Graduate Diploma in Theological Studies in Laidlaw College. My wife studied Diploma of Counseling and a Graduate Diploma at Laidlaw College. My sons also studied in Auckland before moving on to Otago University.

My eldest son, Joseph and my second son, Joshua did very well in high school. Joseph and Joshua both became Dux scholars of Mount Albert Grammar School. The school teachers were very happy because good students brought good reputation and goodwill to the school.

During one "meet the teacher session", one of the teachers asked me, *"Do have any more sons to send to us?"*, and I responded, *"Yes, I have one more!"*

In fact, my youngest son, Joel was also a top student in Glendene Primary School. A few years later Joel studied in a high school in Dunedin where he too became a Dux scholar. I thank God for my three intelligent sons. All glory to God.

Throwback Photo – My three sons and I

HONOR GOD AND HE WILL HONOR YOU

Studying in the Bible college was the best thing that had ever happened to me. I felt so blessed to be a living sacrifice for the Lord. On the first day of class, I vividly remember one lecturer addressing the class, *"For the next one year, do not think of any other thing. Devote the next one year fully to God. Give all that you have to God. He will honour you if you honour Him"*.

In Bible college, I learned how to write academic essays with bibliography and footnotes. I learned how to write research papers, and utilise library resources for self-learning and assignments. Additionally, I was also trained to think critically, theologically, and logically.

GRADUATING WITH TWO DIPLOMAS

I had to attend lectures and pass examinations for every single module. Apart from academics, I also had the opportunity to make friends and build meaningful relationships with other students.

My time here passed rather quickly. After three years of studies, I graduated with both the Diploma of Graduate and Post Graduate Diploma in Theological Studies and attended two graduation ceremonies – one for each Diploma.

TWO SAD INCIDENTS

There were two sad incidents during my time at the Bible College. One student who was suffering from depression committed suicide by carbon monoxide poisoning. He sat inside his car, started the engine and locked himself inside a closed garage.

Then there was the unexpected death of the late Brian Harthaway, the then principal of Laidlaw College. One morning, he went out for his usual morning jog, collapsed due to a heart attack and passed away. He went home to be with the Lord having finished his race here on earth. May his soul rest in peace.

A TRULY ENRICHING EXPERIENCE

Life in the Bible College was truly enriching. I was taught by prominent Bible scholars and pastors. I studied theology, exegesis, hermeneutics, spiritual formation, preaching, evangelism, biblical books, mission, pastoral care, etc.

I made friends with students from Malaysia, Singapore, Hong Kong, Taiwan, Korea, Indonesia, Fiji Islands. We worshiped in the Kelston Community Church, KCC, and participated in church life there. The pastor of KCC was also a lecturer at Laidlaw College. We had frequent potluck dinners organized by the Kelston Community Church and Bible College.

The highlight of the Bible College was the Marae visit. The Marae is a community meeting place of the Maori communities that is unique to New Zealand. It is a complex of carved Maori buildings enclosed within a fenced or gated area.

Every Maori tribe or whanau has its own Marae. We spent 2 days and 1 night in a Marae in Auckland. We learned about Maori history and culture, flex weaving, traditional Maori songs and dances, the Haka, and enjoyed authentic hangi lunch and dinner.

We slept overnight in a big community hall with individual floor mattresses for all participants. Participants sang Christian songs and shared testimonies late into the night until everyone fell asleep. In the middle of the night, I remember being awakened by some of the students who were snoring very loudly.

There was a big Asian community in the Bible College, We formed our own Asian Christian Fellowship which consisted of Asian students from Malaysia, Singapore, Hong Kong, China, Taiwan, Japan, and Korea. The Japanese and Korean students were very weak in English and they had great difficulty writing essays. We had weekly lunch meetings and monthly pot luck dinners.

One female Japanese student was a professional hairdresser. She gave us some excellent hairdressing tips for both men and women while demonstrating her skills. I once volunteered to have my hair cut by her, and that was surely the best the haircut I have ever had in my whole life! We also had classes in car maintenance and cooking as some of the Bible College students were accomplished mechanics and chefs.

SOJOURN IN WELLINGTON

After that, I spent 2 years in Wellington as a medical doctor, working as a Senior Registrar in Internal Medicine and Cardiology, but my wife and youngest son stayed back in Auckland. By then, my two older sons were already studying at the Otago University in Dunedin – the oldest in Medicine and the younger in Dentistry.

I worked in one year in Masterton Hospital and another year in Wellington Hospital. I was also involved as a committee member of the New Zealand Overseas Trained Doctors Association (NZOTDA).

This was a grouping or "union" of overseas trained doctors in New Zealand whose degrees were not recognized by the New Zealand Medical Council and therefore could not practice medicine in New Zealand.

Many of them became taxi drivers, real estate agents, staff nurses and so on. Through the Association's collective efforts in lobbying politicians, the Medical Council and making our voice heard through the press and other media, many of our members succeeded in getting provisional registration and hospital positions.

A significant number of our members also migrated to Australia where they were able to get provisional registration and hospital positions much more easily.

GOD'S HAND OF PROVISION

It was God's intervention that enabled me to be able to practice medicine in New Zealand where it was almost impossible for foreign graduates to become registered medical practitioners at the time. My medical degrees were not recognized by the Medical Council of New Zealand.

But I prayed and fasted, and God eventually answered my prayer. I met a Professor of Medicine at the University of Wellington and with his recommendation, I was able to get a provisional registration where I was required to work under supervision by a fully registered medical specialist who had to sign me up every year.

After 2 years in Wellington, I decided that New Zealand was not the place for me to stay in the long-term and I made the decision to return to Malaysia when my contract ended.

REMEMBERING 9/11

I was in Wellington on the morning of the terrorist attack on 11th September 2001 when flight 175 crashed into the Twin Towers of New York. I was having breakfast and watching the television news broadcast in the doctor's lounge when the footage of the 9/11 incident was shown on television. At first, I thought it was a new Hollywood Box office movie release until the news reader said that it was real – non-fiction! I was shaken to the core and so were my colleagues.

BACK AGAIN IN IPOH

In 2003, after 5 years in New Zealand, I moved back to Ipoh, Malaysia with my wife and my youngest son. My two older sons stayed back in New Zealand to pursue their own careers, one as a medical undergraduate and the other as a dental undergraduate student.

In Ipoh, I joined the Perak Community Specialist Hospital as a Resident Cardiologist and Physician, and KPJ Ipoh Specialist Center as a Visiting Cardiologist and Physician.

Private practice in Ipoh was demanding and labour intensive. I had to manage a very busy outpatient clinic. Then there were cardiology procedures to do, invasive, non-invasive, interventional, and emergency procedures. I had to be on call 24/7. My REM sleep was frequently interrupted, and I was also exposed to a lot of radiation – which took quite a toll on my health.

My social life was severely disrupted. Time management was important to avoid burning out. Every few years, I would take substantial time off from my work as a form of sabbatical leave to rewind, recharge and regain balance – to ensure that I did not burnout. For me, at this juncture, studying in the bible college was a form of sabbatical leave.

A CALLING, NOT JUST A CAREER

The nature of my work was such that I would be called up in the oddest hours of the day to attend to patients. When everyone was asleep, I would be working.

I viewed Medicine as my calling – not just a career

There were many times I was called up from 3am to 7am to attend to patients and I had to be back at work again by 9am that very same day! This was and is part and parcel of a doctor's life. To me, it was always more than a career or vocation – it was a calling and a passion!

Perhaps to some degree, my only regret is that I did not have more time to bond with my sons as they were growing up. But I remember telling bible stories, including one of favourites – David and Goliath, to my youngest son Joel every night before he went to sleep.

Now that they are all adults and have their own children, they are not very close to me. If I have the chance to go back in time, I would like to do it differently. But God willing, there will still be the chance to do it right again with my grandchildren.

In the course of my private practice, I was also a marketplace soul-winner. I shared the gospel with many of my patients using my office as a pulpit.

Consequently, many of them came to know Jesus Christ as Lord and Saviour as I led them to recite the sinner's prayer. For patients who were already Christians, I prayed for them whenever they came to see me.

In Ipoh, we attended the Holy Cross Lutheran Church. We also signed up for weekly Bible seminar classes which were taught by an anointed Pastor from Kuala Lumpur.

We followed him through the book of Genesis to the book of Revelation – a very in-depth study of the entire 66 books of the Bible, over a span of 16 years. This gave me a very solid exegetical and hermeneutical foundation of both the Old and New Testaments.

PILGRIMAGE TO THE HOLY LAND

I also accompanied this Pastor on pilgrimages to the Holy Land twice – in 2005 and 2019. Amazingly, the Bible just came alive when I visited key places mentioned in the bible.

The places of pilgrimage included Sea of Galilee, Mount Carmel, Bethlehem, Joppa, Mount of Olives, Western Wall, Shiloh, The Temple Mount, City of David, Magdala, Capernaum, En Gedi, Via Dolorosa, Garden Tomb, Gethsemane, Church of the Holy Sepulcher, Temple Institute, Hezekiah's tunnel, and the Pool of Siloam, among others.

Sea of Galilee – Holy Land Pilgrimage 2019

Mount Carmel – Holy Land Pilgrimage 2019

After returning from the Holy Land, I feel that the bible comes alive whenever I read and study it even to this day – after all, isn't God's Word *"Living and Active"* as Hebrews 4:12 declares? Over the past 16 years, I have had the opportunity to preach in three local churches once every 6 to 8 weeks.

In Bethlehem – Holy Land Pilgrimage in 2019

Golan Heights – Holy Land Pilgrimage in 2019

TUNG LING SEMINARY

My wife and I also studied at the Tung Ling Seminary, Ipoh. We enrolled for night courses over 3-years as audit students. These courses were conducted by lecturers from Tung Ling Seminary, Kuala Lumpur for 6 weeks once a year.

2014 in Barcelona for the ESC Congress

At the European Society of Cardiology

With my wife in Mumbai

Visiting Edinburgh

With Prof. Eugene Braunwall – "Great-Grandfather" of Cardiology

We attended these classes from 6pm until 10pm. They were conducted in the form of lectures, workshops, assessments, and examinations. My wife and I also travelled locally, regionally, and internationally for medical seminars and conferences as part of continuing medical education (CME) for renewal of my yearly annual practising certificate.

In Mumbai with Dr. Spencer B. King,
Ex-President, American College of Cardiology

Over the many years of medical practice, I was awarded Fellow of the Academy of Medicine Malaysia, Fellow of the National Heart Association of Malaysia, Fellow of the American College of Chest Physicians, Fellow of the Asean College of Cardiology, and Fellow of the Asian Pacific Society of Cardiology.

Convocation – Fellow of the ASEAN College of Cardiology

GOD'S CONSTANT FAITHFULNESS

My wife and I also travel yearly to Auckland and Dunedin in New Zealand, and Melbourne in Australia to visit my sons, daughters-in-laws, grandsons and granddaughters.

My wife & I – At our 40th Wedding Anniversary on 31st August 2017

Picture Perfect – with our Grandkids

ve

grandsons and four granddaughters. By the grace of God, my family grew from just two persons in 1977 to fourteen in 2020!

I can testify beyond any shadow of doubt that my God is a good God. He has faithfully looked after me and my family through the years, taking me through the best of times and the worst of times.

Family Portrait – Fruitfulness & Multiplication by God's Grace

Family Portrait – A Constant Reminder of God's Faithfulness

BOBBY

A dog is indeed a man's best friend and I had a dog in Ipoh too. He was an Alsatian-Mongrel mixed breed. I also called him Bobby, the same name as my other dog in Tanjong Malim. I got him when he was only a puppy.

One day, a cobra entered into the compound of my house. Bobby was very brave. He saved the day. He barked and guarded the compound and prevented the cobra from entering into our house. I quickly called the "Bomba" (Fire-Rescue Squad) for assistance. They sent a team over to my house and safely removed the cobra. I was forever grateful to Bobby for this act of selfless courage. After about 9 years, Bobby became very old and frail.

One day, when it was raining heavily, I opened the gate, and Bobby rushed out of the house. I could not get him back into the house because of the heavy rain. I thought he would come back later but he did not.

Every day, my wife and I would comb the neighbourhood with our car to look for Bobby, but he was nowhere to be found.

Three days later, we spotted him lying down in a field looking weak and frail. We took him into our car, brought him home and looked after him. However, Bobby passed away peacefully after several days. I buried him in the compound of my house. I was very sad, but thank God, I found him and had closure over the incident. Otherwise, I would still be feeling guilty.

DOWN BUT NOT OUT!

Locked down but not out,
Knocked down but not out!

Chained to the house,
But not to the ground.

Chained to ipad and imac,
Mind soared upon high.

Covid-19 on the rise,
Vaccine arise and shine!

CHAPTER EIGHT

RETIREMENT & *TESTIMONY*

"A dream, all a dream, that ends in nothing, and leaves the sleeper where he lay down, but I wish you to know that you inspired it."

- A Tale of Two Cities, Charles Dickens.

On 26th December 2019, I attended a post-Christmas, pre-

New Year celebration dinner with my cardiologist colleagues in a hotel in Ipoh.

THE ACCIDENT

After dinner, when I was leaving the restaurant, I tripped and fell. I cannot quite remember how I fell. I must have momentarily lost consciousness, and when I came to myself, I saw my friends looking at me and calling out to me.

I could see and hear them, but I had a strange feeling. I could not feel my body from below the neck, and this was frightening! It was as though my head was cut off from the rest of my body. I could not move my hands and feet. I had no sensation whatsoever below my neck. It dawned on me then that I was a tetraplegic – the fall must have resulted in neck injury and spinal shock.

My colleagues called for an ambulance and transferred me to KPJ Ipoh Specialist Hospital. The paramedics were very careful not to move my neck and protected it with a cervical collar. I was immediately taken for an emergency MRI brain and neck scan and subsequently admitted to the ICU.

The MRI scan showed no head trauma, but there was a prolapsed intervertebral at the C3/C4 level causing a 90% compression of the spinal cord, confirming the diagnosis of a prolapsed intervertebral disc with cervical myelopathy at the C3/C4 level. By then, it was already past midnight.

THE SPINAL SURGERY

The next morning, I was taken for a CT scan of the neck to delineate the prolapse intervertebral disc in more detail. By then, the spinal shock had resolved but I was still tetraplegic. The spinal surgeon who attended to me advised urgent spinal cord decompression surgery to remove the prolapsed intervertebral disc and to decompress the spinal cord.

He explained that this was a delicate and precise operation, and indicated that there was a risk of permanent spastic tetraplegia in the event of complications arising during the operation. At 8pm on 27th December 2019, I was wheeled into the operating theatre for my scheduled operation. I heard the anesthetists in attendance saying that they were giving me pure oxygen, and will be putting me to sleep.

REHABILITATION & RECUPERATION

The next thing that I remember was the doctors calling my name, asking me to wake up, saying that the operation was over. When I opened my eyes, I saw the doctors, nurses, paramedics, and the clock in the operation theatre – indicating that it was 11pm.

I was wheeled back to the ICU. After eight days in the hospital, I was well enough to be discharged on a wheel chair. After six more weeks of outpatient physiotherapy and rehabilitation, I finally recovered and was discharged from physiotherapy.

At that time, the Covid-19 pandemic kicked in, and the whole country was under lockdown. It took me another two months more before I became fully ambulant. It is now 12 months after my operation, and I am fully ambulant.

THANKS FROM A GRATEFUL HEART

I truly want to thank God for saving my life. He rescued me from spinal shock and spastic tetraplegia. God also saw me through the successful spinal surgery and post-operation rehabilitation. My gratitude to all my cardiologist colleagues for calling the ambulance and protecting my neck during the ambulance transfer.

I also want to thank my wife, my sons, my daughters-in-law, my sister, my nephew, my relatives, my in-laws, my friends, my colleagues, my pastors, my church members, my school classmates, and my university classmates for their support. And I am very grateful for all those who prayed for me, cared for me, visited me, cooked for me, bought food for me, supported me, encouraged me, and reassured me.

And finally, I want to thank the spinal surgeon, neurosurgeon, neurologist, anesthetists, radiologists, staff nurses, nursing aides, paramedical staffs, radiographers, physiotherapists, KPJ ISH hospital directors, and all the other hospital staff, who attended to me during my hospitalization.

NOTHING SHORT OF A MIRACLE

According to one of my cardiologist friends who was with me during the dinner, and who was an eye witness to the accident, I fell with my head facing downwards hitting the floor, and I seemed lifeless for about 2 to 3 minutes. He said that at that moment, he thought I had died and was very worried for me. Fortunately, I revived spontaneously.

According to my eldest son, who is an anesthetist in New Zealand, injuries such as this almost always result in permanent tetraplegia. He is convinced that my complete recovery in such a short time is indeed a miracle.

LIVING IN THE GOODNESS OF GOD

So many people prayed for me, through WhatsApp messenger and in person. My wife and sister were very supportive throughout my hospital stay and post-operation. My in-laws were also very supportive throughout my ordeal. They drove me to various places outside Ipoh during the Chinese New Year of 2020 for food and recreation, just to cheer me up.

I thank God for preserving my life so that I can continue to serve Him. God is good! His love, compassion, mercy, and grace were lavished on me. God's eyes were on me throughout my ordeal – I experienced such amazing grace. Once I could not walk but now can walk! I hope this testimony will be an encouragement for you as it has been and continues to be for me.

RETIRED & REFIRED

On 11th January 2020, I celebrated my 68th birthday. It also marked the day I hung up my stethoscope for good and promoted it into a museum piece, after 48 years of practicing medicine. I resigned from my position in Perak Community Specialist Hospital and KPJ Ipoh Specialist Hospital and officially retired from medical practice for good.

After retirement, I began serving the Lord in St. Andrews Presbyterian Church Pengkalan, Ipoh, as a lay preacher, bible teacher, worship leader, and bass guitarist. I also became an author and self-published several books. Retirement gave me the time that I needed to do the things I previously could not do.

Over the past 12 months, I have authored 8 books including Expository Commentaries on the Gospels of Matthew, Mark, Luke and John, Acts of the Apostles and Romans, Expository Preaching, Daily Devotions from the Gospel of Mark, and Memoirs of a Doctor.

I wish to praise My God for His abundant blessings that He has bestowed upon me and my family.

Postscript from Grandma Wai Yin

To my family, when the children behave "silly", they are at their cutest. Look at the kittens and the puppies – they are so "silly" but so cute that you cannot help falling in love with them.

This is the same as with the children. What you find "silly" in them is actually so cute that grandparents will keep in their hearts and remember always. For these "silly" things are exactly what makes us lose our hearts to them and love them.

The little ones are precious gifts from God. Some things that you think are naughty things are just innocence and childishness. Please read this memoir to your little ones even as I will do the same to mine because I love them so much.

God bless you!

Grandma Wai Yin
February 2021

Epilogue

It remains for me to pen an epilogue to add in a few things that I may have missed out and to tie up loose ends to draw my memoir to a close.

In this memoir, I have attempt to present the key events of my life story beginning from my birth in 1952 until my retirement in January 2020 – covering a span of 68 years. I did not attempt to cover all aspects of my life events as this is far beyond the scope of this book.

Some of the events described may not be one hundred percent accurate due to the long-time lapse. As such, and should that ever be the case in any instance, I wish to apologize for any inaccuracies or omissions.

I remembered that during my growing up years in Tanjong Malim, many European missionaries came to evangelize to the town people. These were usually husband and wife teams who came to live in Malaysia and even learnt the local Chinese dialects and the Mandarin language.

They shared the gospel by using a portable black board and chalk to explain the gospel story. After the presentation, they would show us a movie using a portable projector and screen. This usually occurred in the evening after dinner. I liked to attend these road shows mainly because of the movies.

After my retirement in January 2020, the Covid-19 pandemic which started in Wuhan, China escalated to alarming proportions and went global. Malaysia was not spared the agony and the country was on lockdown since March 2020. At the time of my writing this epilogue today in February 2021, the vaccination program is expected to take off soon in Malaysia. Hopefully, with the vaccination program, the pandemic will be over soon to alleviate suffering and anxiety.

During the past year, I have managed to redeem the time by writing books and by the grace of God, managed to self-publish two books in Amazon KDP. This third book is the result of many hours of laboring behind the computer and word processor.

My journey in writing has taken me to uncharted territories which were quite beyond my imagination. Along the way, I have acquired new skillsets, new knowledge, new friends, new vocation, and new perspective. Most importantly, God was with me – guiding me, teaching me, and helping me along this book writing journey.

Finally, I wish to end "Memoirs of a Doctor" with a quotation from Isaiah 40:26, *"Look up into the heavens. Who created all the stars? He brings them out like an army, one after another, calling each by its name. Because of his great power and incomparable strength, not a single one is missing".*

2020 – THE YEAR IT WAS

2020, a year of writing,
unleashing the power of healing.
A year of substantial learning,
new writing skills for acquiring,
new methodology notwithstanding.

2020, a year of the mighty pen,
writing to inform, teach, and plan,
to convict, correct, train, and send,
reaching out to the mass.

2020, a year of blogging,
3000 followers and counting,
A year of unimaginable suffering,
For everyone who is living.

Andrew C.S. Koh ©2021

About the Author:

Dr. Andrew C.S. Koh is a retired cardiologist who lives in Ipoh, Perak, Malaysia. He studied Theology and graduated with Graduate and Post Graduate Diplomas in Theological Studies from Laidlaw College, Auckland, New Zealand in 2001.

He worships at St Andrew's Presbyterian Church Pengkalan, Ipoh, Perak, Malaysia. He is an accomplished author, poet, musician, lay preacher, bible teacher, expositor and soul winner.

Made in the USA
Monee, IL
22 March 2021